SPIRITUAL SURVIVAL GUIDE

FOR PRISON AND BEYOND

FRED NELSON

The Inside Out Network
Park Ridge, Illinois

ionillinois.net

INSIDE OUT
ion
NETWORK

Edited by David A. Zimmerman

Cover and interior design by Rebecca Larson

Logo design by Thor Uremovich

ISBN: 978-1-4675-2429-2

Portions reprinted and adapted with permission.

To request more copies of *Spiritual Survival Guide* please contact

The Inside Out Network
1006 Gillick St.
Park Ridge, IL 60068
ionillinois.net

Contents

Introduction   5
How to Use This Book   8

1. Starting Well: Surviving Spiritually on the Inside   10

Voices from the NRC: Changing Your Life and Connecting to God   13
How People Change (or Don't)   19
What Works and What Doesn't: Wisdom from C and D Blocks   25
From Where I Sit (Chaplain George Adamson, Stateville Prison)   28

2. Read This If You're Confused
About Faith, the Bible, Prayer, and All That   32

Why Jesus?   33
Why Grace?   35
Belonging and Believing   38
Questions People Ask About the Bible   44
The Big Love Story   48
Reading the Bible   55
Ten Words That Could Use Some Explaining   57

3. Forgiveness   60

Love's Toughest Work   62
The Heart and Art of Forgiveness   64
When It's Really Hard to Forgive   66

4. Shame   72

Who Are We, Really?   75
From Where I Sit: The Journey from Shame to Joy
(Fred Nelson, Pastor)   77

5. Complicated Stuff   88

You, Addiction, and God   89
From Where I Sit: You, the Gangs, and God (Various Inmates)   96
Maintaining (or Regaining) a Meaningful Relationship with Your Family   103

From Where I Sit: What It's Like for Me When You're Locked Up
(Family Members of Inmates)   115
Being a Man, Being a Father   117
From Where I Sit (Tom Beatty, Head of the Malachi Dads Program)   123

6. Keeping It Going: Moving Beyond Survival Mode   127

Biggest Challenges and Frustrations   128
Biggest Surprises and Joys   138
Prayer Life: Top Ten Things We've Learned   142
Prayers That Made a Difference   152
Praying Your Own Prayers   158
Walk Like a Christian: 12 Steps Toward Thriving Spiritually   161
From Where I Sit (Dan, Former Inmate)   178
Inmates Share a Month's Worth of Spiritual Advice   182

7. Surviving Spiritually Beyond Prison   190

"What Happened When I Got Out": Dan's Story   191
Hope and Realistic Expectations   194
Planning and Communicating   202
From Where I Sit: Preparing Yourself for Re-entry (Mary Johnson,
Prison Fellowship)   204
Surviving Spiritually at the Speed of Life   209
From Where We Sit: Advice from Former Prisoners   218

8. Bible Studies for Inside and Out   220

Alive Again: Prodigal Son, Prodigal Love   224
Prisoners in the Bible: I Was in Prison   230
Prisoners in the Bible: Cain and Abel   236
Prisoners in the Bible: Joseph in Prison   242
Prisoners in the Bible: Peter in Prison   246
Prisoners in the Bible: Paul and Silas in Prison   252
Prisoners in the Bible: Freedom for the Captives   258

Final Thoughts and a Prayer   262

INTRODUCTION

You still have time.

You're still breathing. Your heart is still beating. You're a *survivor*. You've been through a lot, but somehow you're still alive and kicking. And so is God. And that's what counts.

It doesn't matter who you are. It doesn't matter what you've done or failed to do. *Seriously.* It doesn't matter if you've been pushing God and "spiritual stuff" away your whole life. Because you still have time. There's still hope. Hope you can count on. Even now, right where you're sitting and reading this. Even in the midst of the chaos around you.

Maybe you're thinking, *I'd like to believe that, but I don't want to be a fool or a phony.* We know the feeling. We've all gone through that same struggle. And believe us when we say that none of us wants to play make-believe, either. That's not what this book is about.

Spiritual survival isn't about faking it. If it was, we wouldn't bother. We wouldn't waste our time—or yours.

But here's the thing: We've learned—some of us the hard way—that we're dealing with a second-chance, hundredth-chance, thousandth-chance God. And because of that amazing truth, *you still have time.* You and God aren't finished writing the story of your life. In fact, you and God can start writing the next chapter of your life. And you can start now.

That's where this book comes in. The first thing we want this guide to do is to fire up your hope that you can not only survive in prison but actually thrive spiritually.

Only God can write the story of our life.
—Melvin

We understand how this might sound as you sit and look around your cell. We know that you've already lost so much. So many broken dreams. So many things taken away. But some things still remain. And one thing you now have in abundance is *time.*

Let that reality sink in: *You still have time.* Time you may not have had on the outside. Time enough to finally pay attention to your soul, your spirit, your deeper self (whatever you want to call it). Time enough to finally get real with the living God who won't let you go—no matter how many times you've ignored him or pushed him away.

A Quick Word About Us

Who we are.

We're basically a bunch of church folks with a mission to create some helpful resources and to connect inmates and returning citizens to God, each other, the local community, and the local church. Over the years we've created two ministries that share that same passion – Under the Door (prison ministry) and Inside-Out Network (reentry ministry). As our vision has evolved, we've shifted focus toward working hand-in-hand with people both inside and outside of prison. That's why we're changing our name to the Inside Out Network. We'll continue to produce resources like the *Spiritual Survival Guide*, but we're also hard at work at producing new helpful resources like a 101-session Bible study curriculum for small groups (see chapter 8 for a sample), RED Chicago (a ReEntry Directory for Chicago), and a revolutionary new ION app for a smartphone to help you transition to a new life when you're released.

As you read through this book, you're going to be hearing from lots of different people—current inmates, former inmates, short-termers and lifers. You'll hear from prison chaplains, correctional officers, pastors of ex-inmates, and family members. You'll be hearing from Christians from a wide range of backgrounds. We're different. And we don't always agree on every detail. That's okay. In fact, we think that's a strength. We agree on the main things about our faith, and we're sure that in these pages God has something important to say to you.

We encourage you to use this book in whatever way makes sense to you and God. Resist the urge to just toss it away. On the other hand, don't just swallow what you read. Test what you find here against the Bible— God's Word. See for yourself if what we say rings true and holds up over time. See if it's useful. We don't think that we have all the answers or that we have everything figured out. But we do want to share what we've learned and experienced along the way.

So think of this guide as a tiny handbook to the real book: the Bible. Think of it as a thought-provoker for surviving spiritually on the inside. Use it as a helpful conversation-starter with others who are struggling with the same questions. Use it to take God and yourself seriously. Go ahead and read on. After all, you still have time.

May God bless your time.

Fred Nelson, with inmates of Stateville Prison and friends of Under the Door

HOW TO USE THIS BOOK

This book isn't meant just to be read. It's meant to be used. It's a tool for you, and not just for you but for you and the people you come into contact with inside. We want you to survive spiritually in prison, but more than that we want you to thrive, and as you thrive spiritually the people around you will be affected, and life in prison can get better for everyone. So there are (at least) three ways you can use this book.

Read It by Yourself

Read this book to help you pass time, to center your mind and to strengthen your faith. Read it slowly, taking time to think about what you're reading and what it might mean for you. Pray about what you read, asking God to take you beyond what's written to what he wants you to learn about yourself, prison and God.

Read It with Your Celly

There's a lot to think about in this book, and you may want to "think out loud." Invite your celly to read the book along with you, or talk to your celly about what you've read. Ask him what he thinks, how he relates to the stories, the insights from other inmates, the questions. Don't annoy him, but don't assume he isn't interested, either. Your celly might surprise you with what he has to say; you might both be surprised with how life improves for both of you.

Read It in a Group

The chaplain at your facility, like this book, is there to help you survive and thrive spiritually while you're inside. If you earn the respect and trust of the staff at your facility, you may have the chance to read the book with a group of fellow inmates. Together you can grow spiritually and imagine ways to help inmates, prison staff and your loved ones outside have a better life.

However you read the *Spiritual Survival Guide*, we hope it's a good experience for you. Let us know how we can make it better by writing us at

The Inside Out Network
1006 Gillick St.
Park Ridge, IL 60068

1

STARTING WELL
Surviving Spiritually on the Inside

So here you are ...

You're behind bars, which means that you're probably going through some perfectly normal emotions right now—anger, fear, remorse, depression, confusion, resentment, self-loathing, anxiety, defiance, shame, loneliness, feeling empty on the inside, blaming, self-absorbed, feeling wronged, still preoccupied with your case. And probably some others that we can't think of right now.

You might be feeling ashamed, either at what you've *actually* done or because you know that most everyone *thinks* that you did it. You're probably feeling some anger. Thirty percent of that anger and resentment is probably directed at other people or God, while the rest is probably aimed directly at yourself.

> State prison is nothing like county jail. You can't talk to the staff the same way. When you first get here, listen and learn.
> —Dave

Here you are in the state prison system. This is a different beast than the county lock-up. Nobody presumes that you might be innocent. You're now seen as the guilty inmate, period. The system is no longer reaching out to help you in the same way. Here you are being "processed," feeling totally out of control. And not just *feeling* it, either. You don't have any control. You didn't let go of control voluntarily. It's been stripped away. Lights out, inmate. One way or another, you've had to become outwardly submissive to survive.

Here you are, filled with a sense of hopelessness, doubt, and uncertainty. You may be depressed and wondering why God didn't protect you. In fact, you may even have had a new-found relationship with God in county jail. But now here you are—convicted—and you feel let down. "God, you said that you forgave me. Now why this?!"

Here you are with different cellies. Some of them have the baby-bird syndrome, whining incessantly about the small stuff. Some of them won't do well because they keep justifying their way into the next wrong decision. Some of them are vulnerable. Some of them are predators. Some of them are truly innocent, caught up in the wrong place and with the wrong people. Some of them are guilty as charged. Some of them are finally ready for some serious change. Who are these people? And just as importantly, who are you to them?

Here you are, and if you're smart, you're keeping quiet and listening. And watching. Watching for counterfeits. Watching for people who aren't what they appear to be.

Here you are, carrying yourself outwardly like you're tough, but at some level you're probably feeling a certain amount of fear. A smart man knows when to feel fear. Fear of physical harm, for sure—things can happen in here any day for trivial reasons. Or fear about what you might have to do to prove yourself. Fear about what the gang might expect you to do for them in here. *Am I expected to have to stab somebody?*

Or maybe you're haunted by a nagging fear about losing your relationships with your people on the outside.

In fact, speaking of family and friends, you may already be feeling a certain amount of rejection and abandonment from them. And for that, you may already be feeling a certain amount of resentment in return. You may have overdone things while you were in lock-up—demanding things from them, basically telling them to *take care of me. Now!*" And that didn't exactly go over too well, did it?

So here you are. Lying on your bunk, hitting the rewind button on your life. Replaying your past, over and over again. How far back are you rewinding the tape? To the night it supposedly all went wrong? Or are you rewinding a lot further back than that? "I know I was told things again and again as a kid, but I wouldn't listen. *Why wouldn't I listen?*"

Here you are. Like most of us who are finding our way through this system, you're probably totally self-absorbed *and* thinking that you're not worth anything. You're simultaneously focused on the man in the mirror, and angry and disappointed and fed-up with the face looking back at you.

And here you are with a "Spiritual Survival Guide" in your hands. How strange is that? Maybe you're a Christian. And even if you're not, you've probably have had some passing acquaintance with God, with the Christian message, with the way of Jesus. Maybe you weren't brought up in a very religious family, but you probably have an aunt or uncle, a grandmother, or someone in your circle of family and friends that was a Jesus follower. Maybe you never had much time or interest in all that. But you're here now, and maybe that door can finally begin to open for you. You're reading, because you want to survive. Good choice. Keep reading . . .

Voices from the NRC: Changing Your Life and Connecting to God

Any way you cut it, the NRC is one strange place. Every time we volunteer chaplains step inside the Northern Reception Center at Stateville Prison, we find ourselves filled with seriously mixed feelings. On the one hand, the facility is bright, clean, modern, organized, and almost silent—a welcome contrast to the century-old, hectic, uncomfortable and noisy maximum-security facility next door. On the other hand, the NRC feels strangely cold and antiseptic, impersonal—not really a place for human beings. And in a very real way, it isn't. It's not meant to be. It's a transit point, a "place-in-between"—a scheduled stopover on the trip from conviction and sentencing to the new prison assignment.

By its very nature, the NRC inevitably has a kind of "warehouse feel" to it. Its purpose is to receive and process inmates who've just been convicted and who need to be assigned to a new prison. So it's little wonder that many of the men who pass through it tend to "zone out" while they're there. They're being "processed," after all. The truth is, there's a lot of depression. With no windows to clue them into the rhythms of the sun, guys tend to sleep *a lot*. With heavy steel doors making cell-to-cell conversation difficult, life tends to turn inward.

And yet, it's not all dreary. Here and there we see signs of life and vitality—like lights in a dark place. As we make our way around the nearly silent hallways with our carts of books and Bibles to hand out, we're sometimes struck by the contrast between the cells where the lights are switched on and where the lights are switched off. It's like day and night. *And not only because of the light bulb in the cell.* Sometimes it's like the guys themselves are either "lights on" or "lights out." The lights-out guys are so obviously being pulled down by their depression, anger, despair, fearfulness or regret. It's like they've switched off spiritually.

13

The lights-on guys are struggling with all of the same things—but along with the struggle there are also signs of hopefulness, activity, conviction, purpose, even joy.

My first year in prison didn't go well. I did look for brothers to align myself with to help me find my way back to the Lord. But I found out that they were only "temporary Christians" so that didn't go too well. It made me think that maybe there weren't any real Christians in prison.
—Kentes

My first year in prison was truly a test of my faith. I was still trying to live as if I was in the free world, even though I had been incarcerated three years before coming to prison. What went well is the time I spent reading God's Word and getting comforted by God's promise that he would never leave me or forsake me.
—Donald

The first year the devil had his way. He destroyed and devastated not only my life, but also my loved ones and families. But I had an overwhelming spiritual experience—in the darkest hour, at the point of considering suicide, overwhelmed by the voice of the enemy, saying, "Kill yourself and cheat the state of putting you to death!" But at that moment I was able to say (in little more than a whisper), "Help me, Jesus!" And he did. I can't explain exactly what happened that night in that cell all alone. But it was like Jesus was just waiting for me to tag him in. My predicament didn't change. My circumstances were the same. But my attitude changed ... and so did I!
—Anthony

The very first day I was guided to a Mr. Green, another inmate who for the last four years has kept my feet on solid ground spiritually and helped me grow immensely from time to time. I've seen God work through Mr. Green and I've desired to have God work through me.
  –Nathaniel

My mind was spiritually awakened. I started thinking different—and better! I got to know Jesus and asked him to come into my life. I don't recall anything bad.
  –Kevin

I wasn't living, walking, or anything else in the Spirit in my first nine years here, so nothing went well. I wasn't trying to find out who I was spiritually. I came off the street doing drugs and came to prison to continue that same course.
  –Jacques

In my first year in prison I was very upset with God because I am innocent of the crime I was convicted of. I asked God why he would let this happen to me knowing the truth about my case. So my faith was shaky because I felt like God did not love me. But as time went on my spirit began to change.
  –Rodney

When I first stepped into the NRC (L-2) in July of 2005, I started praying to God that I would be assigned to a prison closer to my family. And God answered my prayer—I came to Stateville. The problem, though, was when I got to prison I was immediately surrounded with unbelievers. That made me totally forget about the blessing that the Lord had just given to me! I now look at the NRC as a holding place of the Lord. He wants you to think first of what you want to do with your time in prison—and that's to do his will.
  –Wilfredo

It was a tough adjustment getting to know the spirit and the persons around you. I'm a quiet guy and like my privacy, so dealing with the new and hurt persons in here was a challenge. I found myself looking for God and asking the ever-resounding question, "Why me and why now?"

    –Earl

I was sentenced to Death Row and at first I was fearful. I ended up making peace with myself and God. I then reached out to make peace with others among my family and friends. I lost some friends because they didn't want to have any more to do with me. But my true friends have stayed around.

    –Robert

My first year in prison I found myself spiritually dead. When I heard the message of Christ I did not accept it. I thought I could continue to lean on my own approach to life and my own understanding. It was not until several years later that I gave my life to Christ.

    –Doaikah

Being a Christian in the free world, walking the walk—or so I thought—I truly felt I was safe from temptation and the devil. So in the beginning I struggled with prison. It turned out to be a blessing of sorts, though. I rid myself from the problems I was going through outside, and being with other Christian inmates helped out tremendously. But let's be honest: evil runs rampant in prisons, and it eats away at my soul to see and hear all the ugliness that continually occurs in here. So many injustices. Always having to pay for the mistakes of others tests a man's faith continuously. It has been hard not to think that we inmates have just been thrown into this warehouse and forgotten by most of society! I've come to believe, though, that God and brothers and sisters in Christ are our only hope! So, what went well? Being put around my Christian brothers that I have encountered thus far has made

prison easier to swallow. It gives me hope for all of humanity when I witness the strong fellowship between brothers in here. What didn't go so well? Being sent so far away from my family and struggling when classes and programs got put on hold or were canceled entirely. Classes and the fellowship through programs give people in here confidence and also self-worth.
  —James

My first year in prison I was just trying to relate to my new environment. I'll be honest: I hated Christians and the Bible. My father sent me books on new age philosophy, psychology, and self-help. At one point the Catholic priest from my parish wrote to me. Surprisingly, I found myself beginning to move in the direction that God wanted.
  —Jose

I thought that because I'd made a decision to live a spiritual life, that all or most of my pain would go away. That didn't happen. I've learned to keep going—one day at a time—doing my best.
  —Dan

What most guys in here need is hope, encouragement. What they need to see is "the walk," somebody showing on a daily basis a different way to live. That speaks the loudest to guys. Only then is a guy eager to hear the "talk," the reason behind the walk. He wants to know the story. "What happened to you? I can see the after. What was the before like? And what made the change happen?" When I tell my story, I tell them that they can think about it a couple of ways. They can think of it as a story of liberation—from "wilderness" (or slave mentality) to "freedom." Or, as a story of healing—from a crippling, cancerous mindset (an internal emptiness) to a healthy mind. And then I tell them that freedom and healing can be theirs, too, if they want it for themselves. They don't have to be defeated by their past.
  —James

As we went cell to cell, there seemed to be some common things we kept hearing. Listening to these guys talk about all the surprising twists and turns in their first year in prison, we realized a couple of important things.

- First, real, long-lasting life change rarely comes quickly, easily, or predictably. True change is often slow, tough, and has its inevitable ups and downs.

- Second, "coming to faith in God" is also slow, tough, and has its own ups and downs.

These two things, "changing our life" and "coming to faith," are essential to spiritual survival. They're deeply connected, but we thought it might be helpful to tackle them one at a time.

Think About It. Talk About It.

1. How do you react to the idea that you still have time and that you and God aren't finished writing the story of your life? With hope and excitement? With skepticism? Why do you think that is?

2. What different emotions have you been feeling lately? For you, what's been the most difficult adjustment as you've entered into the prison system?

3. Do you know guys who seem to be "spiritually switched-on"? What do you think of them? And how would you describe yourself? Switched off? Switched on, but pretty dim right now? Switched on and shining? Are there any spiritually switched-on guys around you right now?

4. Which inmate's testimony that you read do you most relate to? Feel the most motivated by? Why is that?

How People Change (or Don't)

A changed life. Man, that sounds good, doesn't it? In fact, there's nothing more that we want for ourselves than an invitation to a changed and transformed life.

On the other hand, most of the time it seems as if there's nothing more impossible. Most of us are already aware of our own inner resistance and our inability to change. Five words pretty much sum it all up for most people—*last year's new year's resolutions*. Everybody fails at this, inside these walls and outside them. *A lot.*

So, why is it we're so resistant to change? Is it because we're too comfortable, too self-satisfied with how we are? Is it because we don't think there's any real need for us to change? Sometimes, sure. But not always.

For example, what if it were a simple case of "Change or die!"? You may have heard that phrase from your mama, your teachers, your social worker. And it didn't have much impact on you, did it? But what if you were told that you had to have a heart operation and that you'd have to change your lifestyle afterwards (things like diet and exercise) or else you'd die? Do you think that would bump up the odds of you changing the way you live?

Yes? Well, think again. Recent medical research tells us the odds are *9 to 1* that even when it's a case of *change your lifestyle or die*, 90 percent of patients recovering from heart bypass surgery haven't made any significant changes in how they live two years later. When faced with a clear-cut *change or die*, most of us still won't change.

What does that tell us about ourselves? Well, first of all, it tells us that all the usual motivators for change aren't doing their job. Or at least not well enough. Research shows pretty clearly *what doesn't work*.

For example, *a sense of crisis* doesn't motivate over time. Six months after surgery (or after conviction), a "new normal" kicks in. The crisis feeling fades, and so does our resolve to change. We slide back into old habits.

Cold hard facts don't do the trick, either. If they did, lots of us wouldn't be sitting where we are today. We can get all the data in the world—but it's just in one ear and out the other. It's like things just don't register somehow. Or maybe on one level, we actually *know* what we need to do. But on a deeper level—deep in our souls—we don't *care*.

> Especially in the NRC, prison isn't concerned with you getting better. You're being moved through a system. Don't check out! Allow yourself to be moved by God while the system is moving you around.
> —Dave

Fear, of course, can be a powerful motivator—for a while. How many times have we said to ourselves, "That was crazy. Never again!" And then a little while later our denial resurfaces, "Hey maybe that wasn't so bad after all!" Because of the way God has wired us, we can only live with so much fear before we get desensitized to it. And then we slide right back into our same old self-destructive behaviors and thought patterns.

For some of us, *guilt* can be a great motivator. But again, only for a while. The truth is,

> Fear wears off. Chronic guilt turns into generalized anger. —Dan

chronic guilt eats away at us and just gets us even more screwed up and resentful than we were before. And then we just spiral further down. The bigger the burden of guilt we carry with us, the more likely it is that the change in us will only be for the worse.

The truth is, we resist significant change and we continue to live the way we do for one of two main reasons.

First, as a *coping mechanism*, a day-to-day strategy just to muddle through life. "I get high to deal with all the stress." "I need to act aggressively because people won't respect me if I don't."

Second, we resist change because we're *locked into habits and addictions.* "I just can't seem to stop anymore!"

And yet, in spite of all our inner resistance to change, most of us—deep down, maybe all of us—long for something more. It's like God has instilled a hopeful instinct deep inside us that there's more to life –more to us—than we're experiencing right now. And so we yearn for that changed life. For *real* life.

In the Bible Jesus says, "I have come that you may have life, and have it abundantly, to the full" (John 10:10). When Jesus says that, something inside us leaps to attention: *Yes! That's what I want! Real, abundant life! I want what Jesus has, and what Jesus says is for us!* Isn't some part of you dreaming of a life full of purpose? A life full of meaning? A life charged with significance? A life filled to overflowing with the joy of loving God and others—and being loved in return?

So how do we actually get in on this new, abundant life that Jesus came to give us? How do we find the motivation to get into position for real, lasting change? Because if even *"change or die"* doesn't motivate us, then neither will any of the fear-based variations— *"turn or burn"* or *"shape up or else."* Or at least they won't motivate us for very long.

Apparently, we need an entirely different approach from "change or die." We need something that can almost completely flip the odds in our favor. And the research tells us that there actually is a different approach where the odds of that happening are *8 to 2.*

In one group of heart bypass patients, 80 percent changed their life-style—for good. Researchers discovered four key motivators and behaviors that worked for them. They actually echo what the Bible has been suggesting and inviting us to all along.

Put on new lenses. Have you ever worn somebody else's glasses—especially if the lenses were thick? If so, you know how distorted, weird, and crooked things look. You feel that the world itself doesn't look quite right. Sometimes it can make your head hurt. You feel unbalanced and dizzy. The only cure, the only sensible thing to do, is to take the lenses off. And the reason is simple—they're not meant for us. Leave them on long enough, though, and even though they don't help you see, you get used to having them on.

The same thing happens spiritually. We borrowed lenses from the dysfunctional world around us—the streets, drug users, screwed up people in our lives. Somehow, along the way, we got used to wearing them, even though they distorted our view of reality and made us unbalanced. After a while we forgot that we were even wearing them. We adjusted ourselves to a messed-up view of reality. Look around and see where those lenses have gotten you. The only cure, the only sensible thing to do is to take them off. And the reason is simple—they're not meant for us.

> In the Bible Jesus says "Here I am." Keep an eye out for God at the NRC, at whatever permanent facility you wind up in. God is there, making himself available to you.
> —Dave

The good news is, God has another set of lenses specially made for you. Lenses to let you see past the lies and distortion. Lenses to keep Jesus' way of living in front of your eyes. Lenses to keep him in focus, to let him model for us what true living is. Lenses to see your future in his loving and capable hands.

When God gives you new lenses, he also gives you new "frames." You can actually stop seeing your life through the frames of regret, blame, mere survival, despair, or a cruel game. Instead of all those, God helps you see life as Jesus sees it.

For example, you can actually "re-frame" this coming year as 525,600 minutes to be lived abundantly, as God's gift—as a relationship, with joy, and on purpose. Imagine that over the next year, whatever happens with your case, or on the deck, or with your family or with your health—come what may—your trust in God wouldn't waver, but would grow. Imagine being at peace whatever happens, because you would be better grounded in prayer. Imagine picturing what life would be like later this year once Jesus has had his hands on you for a while.

If we're really going to trust Jesus and let him give us new prescription lenses, then we're going to have to remember this, too: *Radical change is easiest.* This is one of the great paradoxes (two things that don't seem to fit together, but actually do) of abundant living.

Here's what usually happens. Most of us try tinkering with our life. We try out small and medium-sized changes for a while. But those small changes usually tend to just make us feel deprived. We give something up, but the payoff seems too small. And so we get discouraged. Pretty soon we start thinking, *Why am I even bothering? Not even this one little change is making any real difference!* And so we stop.

When we try to tinker with all those entrenched habits and addictions of ours, it's even worse. Anybody who's ever spent any time around addiction soon discovers that our attempts to "manage our addiction" are doomed to failure. It's a cruel myth that only sinks us deeper into slavery and makes us despair of ever changing at all. The truth is, we need radical change. We need to let God get his hands on us.

On the other hand, if radical change is ever going to happen, then we need some short-term wins. Since we're an easily discouraged group of people, we need some practical steps that head us in the right direction. We need to have the Holy Spirit help us with some momentum builders, some minor victories, that can feed our faith and combat all the negative voices.

Let's say your vision of living more abundantly this year involves (1) being more disciplined in your prayer life and (2) reading the Bible in a way that gives you more understanding. Your short-term wins might involve deciding that for the next month, you're going try a couple of specific disciplines.

So, for example, you leave your copy of the Bible or other devotional material on top of your toothbrush each evening, and vow not to brush your teeth each morning until after you've gone through that day's texts and said your prayers. You just set your Bible there on top of the brush. It's a simple thing: if you don't pray, you don't brush. It's simple, and it works. (*Unless you like green, fuzzy teeth, that is!*)

Second, you might try your best to get connected spiritually in the next thirty days. You share this book with your celly or another guy on your deck. You ask him if he'd like to read a section and talk over the questions at the end. You get out of your own head for a while without worrying about the outcome. God will take care of the outcome. You just begin to put yourself in those situations where God can do his thing.

In A.A. we remind each other to pray for people we dislike. —Dan

If it's a less selfish and judgmental spirit you feel Jesus calling you to, you might vow to pray for the guys around you for the next thirty days. Not one day more. But not one day less, either. You make a list, starting with your celly (if you have one). You include the guys up and down your deck, and the officers on all the different shifts (even the ones you don't know or can't stand). During this time you keep it to yourself; nobody else needs to know what you're up to. But you'll know. And so will God.

The key thing is, don't try to overwhelm yourself with taking too many steps all at once. That's a recipe for stumbling. At this stage just commit yourself to one month of small, short-term wins. Just get yourself to next month. And then you and God can figure out where to go from there and what steps you'll want to take to get there.

Get ongoing help. If you really want to flip the odds in seeing significant change in your life from *9 to 1 against to 8 to 2 for*, get ongoing help. The research showed that heart bypass patients needed *at least weekly* support and coaching in order for them to stay on track. Otherwise all their health gains tended to unravel.

Think about how many of us are too proud to look for help *once,* much less on a weekly basis! We have to find a way to come out of our isolation, simply for the fact that it's blocking us from changing. We need focus and attention *and helpful friendship.* The truth is, we change best when we change together. That's why you hear the Christian guys around you always talking about "fellowship." It's not about being in some kind of exclusive religious club, or about forming a Christian "gang." It's about being honest and getting that ongoing help that we all need.

What Works and What Doesn't: Wisdom from C and D Blocks

We thought it would be interesting to compare what we were hearing from guys passing through the NRC with what inmates from Stateville said when they reflected back on their first few months. We wondered what they might say about what worked for them and what didn't. What follows is not a list of "dos and don'ts" that you'd better do or else.

This is simply what some guys (Anthony, West, Nathaniel, Duncan, JT, Jose, Dennis, James, Doaikah, Robert, Earl, Wilfredo, Jacques, Dan and others) have experienced in their own lives about what actually works and what doesn't.

When you put the voices from the NRC together with the wisdom from the guys in C and D Block, an interesting picture comes into focus. There are some clear differences between what leads to a dead end spiritually and what actually does work over time.

When you put it all together, you can see some very different paths toward change. One path—the one most of us, both inside and outside prison, normally try—is based on a sense of crisis, cold hard facts, fear, or guilt. That's a path we tend to try to walk alone. Ninety percent of the time it doesn't work; it gets us nowhere. If you like those odds, you're welcome to keep walking that path.

There's another path to a changed life, the path God holds out to you. It's a path marked by new God-given lenses for seeing the world differently, by radical (and exciting) change, by practical short-term victories, and by ongoing help from friends going through the same thing.

The choice, as they say, is yours. God's Word describes it like this:

> I have set before you life and death, blessings and curses. Now choose life, so that you and your children may live and that you may love the Lord your God, listen to his voice, and hold fast to him. For the Lord is your life, and he will give you many years. (Deuteronomy 30:19-20)

Choose life!

What Doesn't Work	What Does Work
Fronting (spiritually and literally)	Being yourself
Trying to fit in, be accepted	Focusing on God
Making yourself out to be more than you are	Fasting
Talking too much	Fellowship with other Christians (inmates, staff, volunteers)
Listening too little	Sharing the gospel with others
Formality	Daily prayer, meditation on God's words
Spouting Bible knowledge without demonstrating God's love	Studying the Bible
Thinking you are better than someone else	Participating in Christian programs, 12-step programs
Thinking that you're so in tune with God that you take the place of God	Exercising the fruit of the Holy Spirit
Holding a cross, Bible, or rosary for good luck or favor from God	Submitting yourself to God
Being stuck in traditionalism	Holding onto God's promises
Isolation or hermit conduct	Talking about personal experiences with people who care and can relate
Avoiding other believers	Hearing other people's stories of life change
Procrastinating	Not getting too discouraged over a lack of results
Endless questioning of God	Forgiving people
Selfishness	Listening to others
Impatience	Showing others you care
Hanging out with people who are not saved	Sacrifice
Worrying too much about what others will think about you	Getting older (it can help you become wiser!)
Treating God like Santa Claus	Sincere confession and repentance
Trying to become perfect	Trying your best to please God above all else
	Promoting God instead of yourself

Think About It. Talk About It.

1. For nine out of ten guys, a sense of crisis, cold hard facts, fear, and guilt don't motivate us over time. Has that been true for you over the years?

2. What do you think about the research that shows that for eight out of ten guys, the four key motivators that lead to deep and lasting change are new lenses, radical change, short-term wins, and ongoing help?

3. What short-term spiritual wins could you try in the next thirty days?

4. When you look at the list of what inmates say doesn't work spiritually, do you see things that you're currently doing? Are you ready to stop doing them?

5. When you look at the list of things that do work spiritually, what two or three things do you think you need to try, or get more serious about?

From Where I Sit:
Chaplain George Adamson, Stateville Prison

Listen to the perspective of a prison chaplain who's met with thousands of guys over the past twenty years, and what he's learned about what it takes to make a strong start spiritual start behind bars.

You are now past the trial and the waiting it out to see which way it would go. You have been transferred to the Illinois Department of Corrections and are now sitting in another waiting

28

period to see where you will be transferred to. On your way to us you undoubtedly thought "WOW! How did I end up here? And how do I get out of here?"

During this time you have been watching, surveying and listening. You have been paying attention to who can be trusted to give you the truth about your situation, who to be careful of, who you can relate to. You've thought, "I have to tell my family what is happening! What about my case? Can I get a lawyer and appeal and win?"

Some of you will be searching for an answer as to why you were not set free. Others will be searching for the ability to adjust to your new life in corrections, be it short or long. Still others will be searching for God.

I believe all things work together for good if you let God have the controls. That means resting in his ability to help and guide you through this process. God is love and as such is a spirit commodity—God can engulf you in such a way that you actually trust him to take you to a life of joy. You can't see it now but God is with you and loves you and desires the best for you. He is not limited by your cage or your circumstances or even your own bad attitude. None of that is any kind of obstacle to him and his desire to grow and bless you.

Surrender is tough for the man who has never done it. It appears to be a weak thing to do. Yet Jesus the Christ surrendered to the cross and died for your sins so that "whosoever believes in Him should not perish but have everlasting life."

You need to make sure you get through the process you are in smoothly and without more trouble. That means surrender to submission—to authority. God has a plan for your life, but so does the devil. If you try to break the system, I'm here to tell you that the system will not be broken any more than it is. The fact that the system exists ought to tell you that it's not going away. You should do your absolute best to get through this process without adding more time to your sentence.

Most of you will run the re-runs of your life. The what-ifs, I-shoulda's, if-onlys … My suggestion to you is to focus on the future. It is where you are headed. Going into it with grief, sadness, anger or fear will not be productive for you. "There is nothing to fear, but fear itself." "Perfect love casts out fear." Soon you will become an expert on your own situation. Entering in with knowledge, understanding and wisdom will go far in your ability to adapt to your new surroundings. Rest in the knowledge that you will survive and be stronger because of it.

The statement of dedication of the Administration Building of Stateville Correctional Center by Rodney H. Brandon, Director of the Department of Public Welfare in 1932, was this:

> Let those who control the lives of the men who enter here ever bear in mind that the path to better things lies upward always and is steep and that God's choicest blessings come to him who helps the weary climber.

You are the weary climber. You will make it to the top if you accept some help along the way. There will be staff who will help you. They are in for God's choicest blessings; you should speak and pray those blessings on them as you go along on your steep climb.

Finally, brethren, whatever is true, whatever is honorable, whatever is right, whatever is pure, whatever is lovely, whatever is of good repute, if there is any excellence and if anything worthy of praise, dwell on these things.
(Philippians 4:8)

2

READ THIS IF YOU'RE CONFUSED
About Faith, the Bible, Prayer, and All That

In case you're wondering, this survival guide doesn't have a bunch of knock-down, drag-out arguments trying to prove that God exists.

It's not that we don't believe that God exists. We do, with every fiber of our being. We're not ashamed of that truth. In fact, we stake our lives on it. Give us a chance, and we might talk to you all day about what we've learned about who God is and how God loves. We're bold but humble—*confident*—about it.

Some Christians specialize in *apologetics*—laying out reasons why you'd be a fool not to believe in their arguments. Most of the time we appreciate their reasons; they can be helpful. But in the end, we don't think arguments about God are enough. (Have you ever known anyone who's been argued into believing in God?)

The Christian message about the reality of the living God is less like an argument and more like a map to share. An argument just goes around and around in endless circles. *"Yes it is. No it isn't. Yes it is. No it isn't."* In an argument nobody has to move or shift their position. A map is different. In fact, "arguing" about a map is pointless. And that's because you can pick up a map and actually test it and experience for yourself. Does it help you figure out where you are? Does it point out the path that leads you home? Does it point out the dangers, the sites of interest, and the twists and turns along the way?

Christians didn't make up this life-map, but we're trying it and it's worth following! This is not a private map. It's for everybody.

> I like when men of faith admit to some doubt. It helps me feel welcome in faith.
> —Dan

There's room for healthy doubt sometimes. But there's room for some healthy faith as well. In any case, God doesn't need us to prove or defend him. He can do that perfectly well for himself. God's an expert at revealing himself. God can and does use Christians to witness to him, to testify and share with others where we've seen him in action in history and in our own lives.

Why Jesus?

You might be asking yourself why there's such a focus on Jesus and the Christian understanding of God in what's supposed to be a "spiritual" survival guide. It's a good question, and a fair one. The main reason is simply because we're Christians. We're followers of Jesus. We're Jesus people. He's our reason for being, our path, our Lord, our way, our truth, and our very life. We can't think "spiritual" without immediately thinking about the Holy Spirit that Jesus sends to his followers.

We're from different "denominations," but not different religions. Think of a house—that's Christianity. Now think of different rooms in that house. Each of those rooms has a slightly different feel to it (Methodist, Baptist, Catholic, Pentecostal, and so on), but it's the same house. We belong to the same family, even if we personally feel more comfortable hanging out in some rooms more than others. We have some minor differences. Like any family, we squabble sometimes. But we belong together. We've got the same head: Jesus.

We recognize that there are other religions, other "houses," than ours. That's immediately obvious in prison. Look around and you can find every kind of religion, and then some!

Many of us have close friends in those other religions. But we're not able to speak for them. That would be inappropriate and foolish on our part. It's hard enough for Christians to speak with one united voice sometimes. How could we ever hope to do that for Muslims, Jews, Buddhists, or any other religious group? It's better to leave that job to people from those communities.

We think that each religion ought to speak for itself and stand or fall on its own. It's wrong to strip away all the distinctive and different ways we see reality. We think that would be untruthful, boring, inauthentic, and unhelpful. There are already plenty of "spiritual self-help" books floating around prison. We're not interested in creating one more.

Why Jesus? We want to offer you an opportunity to meet him yourself for who he really is—and to see what a Jesus-shaped life might mean for you. Atheist, lapsed Christian, Muslim, Buddhist, Satanist, or whoever you are—we don't pre-judge what meeting with Jesus might mean for you. Perhaps Jesus will "confirm and complete" you by bringing to fulfillment all the good and God-pleasing things in your life. Perhaps Jesus will "confront and convert" you by unmasking the lies you live by and showing you his living truth. Perhaps, like us, he'll do all of those things to you.

Why Grace?

Have you ever asked yourself what life's all about? How it all fits together?

Not just your own individual life, but all of it? What makes it all tick? The world? Existence? Everything?

There are two distinctly different ways to talk about what makes it all tick. The first way is earning it. The second way is getting a gift. In the end, it comes down to these two approaches: karma and grace.

The idea of karma is everywhere these days. Karma literally means "action." It's about actions, deeds, works, and the results of those actions, the consequences of what we do—the law of cause and effect. Karma says that actions always have reactions, that things don't happen for nothing, that you get what you give. Karma says that what goes around, comes around. Good actions get rewarded, and evil ones get punished—measure for measure—and if not in this lifetime, then in a whole cycle of lifetimes to come. (Karma's kid sister is reincarnation—coming back around in life after life for the cause and effect process to work itself out. Karma's got a long time-line.)

Settling accounts. Good or bad. Either way, in the end, under karma you get what's coming to you. You get what you deserve. In the end, *you earn it.* Karma says, "Now it's up to you. You've got free will. Create your destiny."

Karma says that whoever you are, wherever you are, whatever level you're on—you deserve it. *You're on top of life?* Well, you deserve it! You must have lived right—either now or in a past life! *You're on the bottom?* Once again, you deserve it. Not-so-good past lives, I guess! *Feeling crushed by life circumstances?* Too bad, but you know: fair's fair. Somewhere in the past, you did this to yourself.

The idea of karma is hard to shake. In fact, the Bible itself wrestles with this payback question over and over. Check out chapters 4 and 34 in the book of Job: when Job's life came crashing down, his friends told him, "You must have deserved this. These things don't *just happen.*"

A karma contingent came to Jesus once (check out the story in John 9:1-7). They asked him, "So, Jesus, is that guy over there blind because he sinned—or because his parents sinned?" Jesus told them, "Don't blame the victims; it doesn't work that way," and then he went ahead and healed the man.

Later (check out Luke 13:1-5), Jesus spoke to his inner circle about people killed in a tragic accident. He told them that tragedies have *nothing* to do with payback. *It's not about who deserves what.* That's not what's going on.

Everything Jesus ever revealed in his teaching, and especially in his cross, is *grace*—us getting wonderful things we don't deserve, and God absorbing the awful things we do deserve. Grace is about God having a soft spot for failures and losers and screw-ups and sinners and addicts and convicts—for all of us who find ourselves on the bottom, and for all of us who *put* ourselves on the bottom.

There's something missing, something out of place, about karma. And there's something deep in our Christian experience, something at the heart of the Christian message, that turns karma on its head. At the heart of Christian experience and identity stands Jesus Christ. And at the heart of Jesus Christ stands the victory of God's grace. Grace is the reality that trumps *everything*. Karma included.

Karma says that life is a "task" to be done and wages to be earned. God's grace in Jesus says that life is a "gift" to be received, opened, enjoyed, and given thanks for. Grace says that because God himself has broken into our world and broken the vicious cycle, history is now going somewhere new, somewhere wonderful. Grace picks up where justice inevitably fails. Clean slate. Fresh start. Debt-free.

Karma says that you are what you make yourself. Grace says that even when we make a total mess of ourselves, God is there to remake us into something new. The Bible says that in Christ we are being remade into a new creation (check out 2 Corinthians 5:17).

Karma says, *Earn it.* Grace says, *Just receive it.*

We've tried to fix ourselves, to play by the rules of cause and effect, but because we're addicted to sin and slaves to selfishness, we can't do it. Thank God we have someone able to fix us. And that's God himself. Thank God we're *not* in control; thank God that he is.

Grace is all about God—in the person of Jesus, through the miracle of a love we can't comprehend—flipping karma on its head, and bringing about a new world order, the kingdom of God. Grace is good news for those who have nothing of their own to point to, for those who have nothing to boast of, for those who don't deserve anything good.

With all due respect to karma, grace rules. Grace is God's first word, God's main word, God's best word, and God's final word. Grace is *amazing*. And grace is meant for people exactly like us.

Think About It. Talk About It.

1. Does the idea that the Christian message is less like an argument and more like a "map" make sense to you? Are you ready to give the map a try?

2. How would you answer the question, "Why Jesus?"

3. At this point in your life are you more drawn to karma (earning it) or to grace (getting a gift)? Why is that?

Belonging and Believing

Maybe somewhere along the way you've run into a preacher or another Christian, and the (uncomfortable) conversation went something like this:

> *"So, have you accepted Jesus Christ as your personal Lord and Savior?"*

> "What do you mean, 'as my personal Lord and Savior?'"

> *"I mean have you, yourself, personally accepted him?"*

> "Yeah, I guess so. I believe he's the Lord of all."

> *"You guess? Okay, but…is he your personal Lord and savior?"*

> "Umm sure, I guess. If he's the Lord of all, then he's the Lord of me, too."

"But have you accepted him?"

"Yeah, I suppose I have."

"What day ... what year ... what happened when you decided?"

"Decided? I'm not sure I ever really decided. I just kind of realized that I believed."

"How do you know for sure if you can't say when? Did you say the sinner's prayer? Did you ask Jesus to come into your heart?"

"Did I do what now?"

Sometimes talking about faith can be like going around in circles. It's like we're talking past each other or speaking different languages. Sometimes, for whatever reason, our answers don't seem to quite satisfy some of our Christian friends. After a while, it can just make us feel stubborn and annoyed, like it's some kind of a competition or something.

Sometimes we get resentful and argumentative, refusing to say the "magic formula" someone desperately hopes we'll say. We won't give them the satisfaction. Why should we? They're not really listening to us!

On the other hand, sometimes we honestly wish that we'd had such a clear spiritual decision day, or some amazing spiritual experience to go back to for strength. Maybe we don't like to admit it, but deep down we feel that there's probably something we're missing out on. If we're honest, and we stop being so annoyed, we can see that our Christian friends are trying to be helpful.

Some Christians look at the Bible and their own lives, and what they see is *believing before belonging.* How can you honestly belong to something (like the church or Jesus), if you don't first believe in it? And how can you believe unless you make a decision to believe? And how could you ever make a momentous decision like that and not know it? That just doesn't make sense. The logic seems to be: no conscious decision, no real faith, no real belonging.

There are a lot of us who do need to make a decision to commit to Christ and his way—people who clearly need a conscious radical break to experience real life change. For whatever reason, some of us just need to be confronted, led by the hand—or dragged kicking and scream-ing—to the moment of decision. Some of us need a clear, conscious radical decision to begin that radical turnaround.

> One way that I try to work out my own unbelief is to pray that God lets me believe as he sees fit.
>
> —Dan

Some of us are like people with serious addictions, whose lives are out of control. Some of us need an *intervention.*

An intervention is like something right out of the Bible. It's like the murderous Saul get-ting knocked on his rear end by a vision of the risen Jesus. For that great story of intervention (it's told three times), check out Acts 9:1-9, 22:1-16, and 26:1-18.

But for every one of us who needs a faith intervention, there's another person for whom intervention and confrontation doesn't quite fit. The world is also full of people who need to come to faith in Christ not in a moment of decision but over a long process. These people start by *belonging* and *experiencing*—and *then* coming to believe.

Some people have trouble trusting any kind of authority or any kind of argument. We need to experience *for ourselves* before we'll commit. That applies to the Christian faith as well. We need to try it on for size, see if feels right, kick the tires, shop around. For some of us, *it's a process.*

That means we've got to be flexible with each other. We've got to meet each other where we are—respect who we are—and lead each other to Jesus down a path that's natural for each one of us. We need to be patient and flexible enough to give people a loving but much-needed intervention when that's called for, as well as giving others enough room to road-test the Christian faith and see that God is real.

That's going to take patience and persistence on everyone's part. Some people make a dramatic decision and then backslide at some point. That's okay—we've just got to be persistent. Others take a really long time getting over their skepticism. That's okay, too. There are no short-cuts when it comes to authentic faith.

Coming to faith in God involves God changing things. First off, God changes us. And then, through us, God begins to change the world. Jesus calls each one of us to be in the world-changing business.

Steve Jobs, the co-founder of Apple Computer, was once trying to lure John Sculley, a top executive with Pepsi Cola, to come and work with him at Apple. He tried all kinds of incentives, but Sculley wasn't going to take the job. Finally, Jobs looked Sculley in the eye and asked him, "Do you want to spend the rest of your life selling sugared water, or do you want a chance to change the world?" Sculley later said that the question knocked the wind out of his sails. It sent his life off in a new direction. *He took the job.*

That's the kind of question you're facing as an inmate: Do you want to spend the next few years doing your sentence, or do you want a chance to change the world?

Every time you lean on the Holy Spirit and help someone find their God-given purposes for living—you change the world.

Every time you help an addicted friend decide to get sober with God's help—you change the world.

Every time you patiently help a skeptic to slowly trust in God, and open up to other people—you change the world.

Every time you write home and help nurture faith in your kids, and they blossom to be the people God destined them to be—you change a life and you change the world.

Every time you challenge men in here to be more generous,

Every time you befriend a lonely person,

Every time you act like part of a community of second-chance people,

Every time you help a celly endure his depression with courage,

Every time you help someone face his sentence with dignity and hope,

God's amazing grace flows, lives are changed, the world is changed, and the kingdom of Jesus Christ advances.

Every time.

Think About It. Talk About It.

1. Have you ever felt pressured by someone else to believe? What happened? How did you react?

2. Are you the kind of person who needs a radical faith intervention (a spiritual kick in the rear end) in order to come to faith? Why is that?

3. Or are you the kind of person who needs time to experience and process things before you can have faith? What made you that way, do you think?

4. Do you want to spend the next few years just doing your sentence, or do you want a chance to get busy changing the world while you're still inside?

When I first started reading the Bible I couldn't see how it related to me or my life. What did God have to do with me being placed in prison? And if God is so forgiving, why doesn't he have me released from prison? At some point I found myself able to read through my "spiritual eyes" and understood how it applied to my life.
—Doaikah

I can't focus on what I'm reading. I know what I'm reading and I know the truth, but my mind tends to wander at times, or I find myself speeding through my reading.
—Anonymous

The Bible shows me how God can and does use all different types of persons: murderers, thieves, liars, and adulterers. Therefore I find myself encouraged that he can use me, too.
—Duncan

I read all the blessings that the Lord did for people and it makes me believe he would do it for me, too. I stopped looking for "big blessings" and started noticing "small blessings."
—Wilfredo

When a Bible verse actually comes to life in your own life—when it answers your current problem, or provides just the word you needed to hear, and seems to be written just for you, that's the greatest thing! It's the father I never had: his stories, history, poetry, wisdom and direction, songs of prayer and praise, scary stories and wonderful adventure—and the guide to teach me to be all I can be with him. To me, it's hope in hopeless times, comfort when I'm alone, strength when I'm weak, correction when I'm disobedient. I'm what it says I am, I can do what it says I can do, and I will become what it says I will.
—Anthony

Questions People Ask About the Bible

Everybody has to start somewhere. And the Bible is a great place to start. Maybe the best. But as you can tell by what other inmates have written, unfortunately it's also a place where lots of us get tripped up. We find ourselves drawn to pick up the Bible, wondering if the living God can communicate with us through it. But then we hesitate to actually start reading it. And so it sits on a shelf, waiting for us.

When we finally do start reading the Bible, we sometimes find ourselves thinking …

It's beautiful. But it's also boring.

It's simple. But it's also confusing.

It's God-filled, and yet so obviously human.

It's life-changing. And frustrating.

It's all of this at the same time!

> I've gotten bogged down in confusion trying to find the messages in the Bible.
>
> —Dan

And so in this section we're going to try to make it a little easier to read and experience the Bible's life-changing message. But first, we know you have nagging questions, places where you're getting stuck. So, let's go ahead and start there.

Well, okay. First off, I see all these different Bibles lying around. Big Bibles, little Bibles. Why so many different Bibles? Which is the real one?

Yeah, it's pretty confusing, isn't it? First off, they're all *real.* They're all worth reading. But in another sense, unless you speak Greek or a few other ancient languages, none of them is *original.*

About three-fourths of the Bible was written in Hebrew. The last fourth was written in ancient Greek. Most of it was written on scrolls, which were about 30-35 feet long and were rolled and unrolled to read. These scrolls were copied by hand by trained readers and writers and passed down through the generations. Because of them we have tens of thousands of copies of different parts of the Bible to compare against each other. So we can be sure that, although we no longer have any of the original manuscripts, these copies we have in English and Spanish are true to the originals.

But between the King James Version, the New International Version, the Gideon's Bible, all of those, which one is the best and most reliable?

Because the original scrolls are in languages that no longer exist, most of the Bibles we see are *translations.* The reason you're seeing all these different versions of the Bible is that there are radically different ways to go about translating something.

Some translators use an approach that is primarily *word-for-word,* taking a word or a phrase from the ancient language and giving its English counterpart. Those kinds of translations are often more formal, stiff, and harder to read. They often don't sound so good in English, but they can be good for research.

Other translators use a *meaning-for-meaning* approach. They're trying to come up with an English translation that recreates the same impact in us that the original Greek would have created for the people who first heard it. Those kinds of translations are usually a lot easier to read and understand in English, but they're not as helpful for serious study.

Given the strengths and weaknesses of each kind of translation, many people like to keep a couple of different English versions of the Bible: one for everyday reading, and one for more serious Bible study.

Whatever version I might have, when I flip through it, it doesn't seem like any other book I know.

On the one hand the Bible is obviously a book; even the word *bible* comes from the Greek word *biblos,* meaning "book." Part of the problem might be what happens when we pick up a book like this one and start reading.

When we were little we were taught to start on page one and read straight on through. There are obviously big advantages to reading a normal book this way. But with the Bible we often run into a lot of confusion and detours. And here's part of the reason why: *The Bible is more like a mini-library than a single book.*

The different sections of the Bible were written by many different people over the course of about a thousand years. Each of these different writers would be inspired by God to share something, and over time the community would add their scroll to the mix. Imagine a box holding all those different accumulated scrolls; that's the Bible.

When it became time to take that box of scrolls and combine them into a single book, they had to make decisions on how to order and group them. And that's part of the reason that the Bible doesn't read as smoothly as a single book written by a single person. There are gaps and overlaps, and a certain amount of jumping back and forth. Keep the image of a boxful of scrolls in mind, and it gets a little easier.

Unpronounceable names. Weird-sounding rituals. Long lists of guys who have been dead for thousands of years. What's that all about?

Maybe you are talking about passages like Numbers 7:78:

> *On the twelfth day Ahira son of Enan, the leader of the Naphtalites: his offering was one silver plate weighing one hundred thirty shekels,*

one silver basin weighing seventy shekels . . . full of choice flour
mixed with oil for a grain offering . . . one young bull, one ram, one
male lamb a year old, for a burnt offering.

Yeah, we feel your pain.

Maybe it can help to start thinking of the Bible not only as a box full of scrolls but also like a *newspaper,* made up of all kinds of different sections. Just flip through and you can find news articles, editorials, letters to the editor, personal ads, advertising supplements, human interest stories, obituaries, comics, menus, stock listings, crossword puzzles, sports, business, advice columns, and so on. In a way, it's a kind of jumble of things.

We don't read a menu, a sports story, and an advertisement in exactly the same way, do we? Not only that, each section of the newspaper is trying to get a different point across to different readers. Once you recognize what section you're holding, it's easier to understand what you're reading.

In the same way, the Bible has a whole lot of different types and styles of writing. About 40 percent of it comes in story (or history) form. But beyond the great stories, there are all kinds of other things: proverbs (wise sayings), songs, poems, parables, letters, visions, genealogies (family trees), prophecies, legal requirements, ancient health and worship regulations, exhortation (encouragement), prayers, meditations, and proclamations (sermons).

Each of these sections has been meaningful to certain people over the centuries. But just like sections of the Sunday paper, not every passage of the Bible will necessarily appeal or apply directly to you right now. That's normal and to be expected.

We've found that the most helpful course of action is (a) to recognize what section we're in, and then, if it doesn't make any sense or seem to apply to us right now, (b) to skip past it for the moment and come back to it at a later time.

It's starting to sound like the Bible is a big puzzle that we have to sort out.

We can see why it might feel sometimes as if the Bible is this bunch of disconnected pieces. But there's something that fits the pieces together, that connects the dots, that organizes all the scrolls into something that makes sense and has incredible power. And that something is an ongoing story running through the whole thing: *an amazing love story between God and human beings.*

But it's a long love story. One website we checked says that the King James Version of the Bible has 783,137 words. That's more than three-quarters of a million words! It's hard to follow the storyline through something that long, especially when it runs from the dawn of creation to the end of time and when the cast of characters keeps changing.

Sometimes, depending on where we are in the story, it can feel like a romantic comedy. Other times it reads like a drama or a tragedy. And sometimes it's just plain crazy and out of control—like an episode of the *Jerry Springer Show.* So what can we do to get our head around the shape of this huge story?

The Big Love Story (the short version)

People who came along before us have found it helpful to come up with a little sketch of the story, or a boiled-down version. Here's one version of the big story, inspired by Rob Lacey's book *The Word on the Street,* that's less than 560 words long.

First off, nothing—nothing but God. And then God's Word rings out, "Let it be!" And it is!

Everything is good, and glorious, and God's. But then, "mess": human sin enters in. Consequences follow, and things go from bad to worse.

God hits re-start and makes big promises to bless humanity through Abraham's family. By God's unearned love the family endures and becomes known as Israel. Later they suffer slavery in Egypt until, under Moses, God shifts into action and liberates them.

They go into the wilderness and enter into a covenant with God. God makes big promises, and the people respond. They manage to enter the Promised Land, but they struggle for hundreds of years. In time, they experience a brief time of life at the top under King David. And then they build a great temple to God in Jerusalem under King Solomon.

But, once again, they melt down in sin. And although God's prophets repeatedly warn the people of their wayward ways, they refuse to change course. The family splits, the nation divides between north and south. They fall and are exiled—and live as refugees far from the land of promise.

But by God's grace, they survive. Eventually some of them return to rebuild the walls and the temple. They see visions of a new day and a new world. They continue to cling to God's promises. And, for 400 years, they wait for God to stir himself to do something new.

And then, in the small town of Bethlehem, God moves in a new and mighty way. The Word of God, the life and light of God, becomes flesh and comes into the world. Jesus is born. And through him all the old story lines connect and all the old promises come into play.

Jesus himself becomes the new way of life, reversing humanity's downward spiral away from God. Jesus completes and corrects the old ways, showing the way of radical forgiveness and holy living, and letting everyone know that God has a new and better future in store.

And, then, when the time of ultimate testing comes, Jesus proves himself obedient to God's will, even to the point of enduring death on the cross. And God raises him up from the dead—canceling the power of sin and death, opening a whole new way of life, and sending his followers out with a worldwide mission to baptize and make disciples of this new life.

Almost immediately, the promised Holy Spirit is poured out, and the church is born. All the barriers between God's covenant people and everyone else are broken down once and for all. The risen Jesus turns enemies into followers. One of them, Paul, becomes the greatest missionary and deepest thinker of them all.

Though persecuted, the Jesus movement continues to grow and spread, as the Holy Spirit fills, guides, and empowers it. It's a life of radical freedom and joy: learning from Christ, living like Christ, trusting in him as our intercessor, grieving with hope, persevering in every circumstance, letting our faith and our works go hand in hand, and keeping Jesus as the Main Thing.

The love story goes on, and includes us all—and reaches

towards the journey's end where God will bring all things to completion and where God will be all in all.

That's one way of putting it. In truth, there are all kinds of ways of telling the story, but sometimes you need to hear the quick version, just so that you get a sense of what's going on. Other times, you want to go over the details and see more of what was going on. We've included a "Bible-at-a-Glance" chart to give you quick look at where any particular passage of the Bible might be in the overall story. Turn the page and see if it helps.

The Bible-at-a Glance

Overview

OLD TESTAMENT

The Beginning

Stories of the creation and our ancient ancestors

History and Law

God's special unfolding relationship with the people of Israel

Wisdom

Wisdom and inspiration for faithful living

Prophecy

God's spokesmen tell it like it is: judgment time and the promise of a new beginning

NEW TESTAMENT

Gospels

The good news about what God has done in and through Jesus

Letters

Reflections on Jesus (who he is and what he's done) and how to follow him in everyday life

The Wrap-Up

A visionary picture of the ultimate triumph of Christ

Details

OLD TESTAMENT

Opening Section

Prehistory:

Genesis 1-11 (stuff starts up and goes from good to bad)

History Section

Genesis 12-50 (from Abraham to Moses)

Exodus (God's people get moving)

Leviticus (a handbook for ancient priests)

Numbers (statistics for those into numbers)

Deuteronomy (contract with God)

Joshua (Promised Land!)

Judges (new leaders for tough times)

Ruth (foreign woman finds faith and a new people)

1 Samuel-2 Chronicles (kings, sex, lies, and catastrophe)

Ezra-Nehemiah (comeback story)

Esther (brave girl to the rescue)

Wisdom Section

Job (a meditation on suffering faithfully)

Psalms (a soundtrack for faith-life)

Proverbs (lessons for living wisely)

Ecclesiastes (dealing with pessimism)

Song of Solomon (a celebration of human love)

Prophetic Section

Isaiah (God's bringing salvation, but at a cost)

Jeremiah—Lamentations (warning signs from a tearful prophet)

Ezekiel (fantastic visions of judgment and new beginnings)

Daniel (visions of God being in control)

Hosea—Malachi (God's "dangerous dozen" tell it like it is)

NEW TESTAMENT

The Good News Section

Matthew (the Good News about Jesus from a Jewish perspective)
Mark (the Good News about Jesus—the shorter version)
Luke (the Good News about Jesus—Volume 1, director's cut)
John (the Good News from a whole different angle)
Acts (the sequel to Luke—Good News, Volume 2: the church starts up)

Letters to Young Churches Section

From St. Paul
  Romans (maybe the greatest letter ever written)
  1-2 Corinthians (Paul writes to some seriously confused Christians)
  Galatians (it's all about freedom)
  Ephesians-2 Thessalonians (who Jesus is and what that means for us)
  1 Timothy-Philemon (personal letters of guidance)

From Other Writers
  Hebrews (looking at Jesus through Old Testament eyes)
  James (practical advice for living the Christian life)
  1-2 Peter (encouraging words for a church facing persecution)
  1-3 John (it's all about love)
  Jude (warning about false preachers)

The Wrap-Up Section

Revelation (a poetic and visionary picture of the ultimate triumph of Christ)

Reading the Bible

Just as there are all kinds of good and helpful versions of the Bible, there are also all kinds of good and helpful ways of reading the Bible. We're going to list six ways that we use personally. Each approach has its own particular strengths and weaknesses, but they're all worth the effort.

Alternate between reading the Bible quickly and slowly. Sometimes it's good to read more quickly through larger chunks. That helps you get into the flow and to make connections. Even if you're not the world's fastest reader, that's okay. Try to read at a pace that keeps things moving along.

On the other hand, sometimes the best thing is to slow it down. Be very deliberate. Read a sentence or two. Focus on what it might mean for you. Then reread it and think through it again. Maybe let it sit with you for the rest of the day. Meditate on it.

Read Jesus first. Often, when asked where to begin reading the Bible, experienced teachers will tell you to start with one of the four Gospels. And here's why: if the heart of the Bible is the love story running through it, then the story of Jesus is the heart of the love story.

The Jesus story is the center of the big story, the key that unlocks the door to everything that comes before or after. From that center, go ahead and branch out. Go back and read some of the Old Testament as a preparation for the Jesus story. Or read some more of the New Testament as a sequel to the main story.

Read it as something spoken to you personally. Ask yourself what God is trying to say to you through these words. What do you need to understand? What do you need to think about more? What do you need to trust? What do you need to get off your chest? What do you need to change? What do you need to ask God for?

These kinds of questions aren't easy to answer. In fact, they're often incredibly difficult. Sometimes they're the very questions that we've been avoiding our whole lives! And yet, it's as if we can hear God speaking directly to us. And there's nothing more exciting—or important—in life than this.

Read it for its plain sense. Depending on the translation you're using, most of what the Bible is saying has a plain and straightforward sense. You don't need an advanced degree to read and understand most of what you'll be reading. And despite what some folks might tell you, you don't need some secret code to unlock the "hidden meaning" in the Bible. God communicates with us in ways that ordinary people can understand.

Read it through historical eyes. You don't need to be a Bible scholar or a historian, but try asking yourself, "What would this have meant to the people who first heard it 2000 years ago? What was going through their minds? What impact would it have had on them?"

These kinds of questions are obviously harder to answer on your own. That's where Bible notes or a commentary can come in really handy. You may be years away from reading the Bible this way, or you may already be deep into this kind of thing. Either way, it has its place.

Read it with others. All of us have both great insights and some weird ideas. When we read and discuss things with others, we're able to share all those good insights and maybe correct some of those weird ideas. That's why Bible study isn't for "fanatics." It's for anybody who wants to understand what they're reading and build themselves and other people up. It can be hard to arrange reading with others in prison, but when you can, try reading together.

Ten Words That Could Use Some Explaining

GOD. People use the word *God* all the time, but they can mean radically different things by it. The Bible has an interesting passage that says,

> Indeed, even though there may be so-called gods in heaven or on earth—as in fact there are many gods and many lords—yet for us there is one God, the Father, from whom are all things and for whom we exist, and one Lord, Jesus Christ, through whom are all things and through whom we exist. (1 Corinthians 8:5-6)

There's a sense that "god" is whatever we ultimately depend on. And for lots of us, our main god is *ourselves.* But beyond all these little gods, there is also the one true and living God.

RELIGIOUS. This word has all kinds of negative associations these days. It can make you think of something impersonal, formal, cold, controlling, and driven by rules and regulations. The original meaning of "religious," though, comes from a Latin word that meant to "connect back," like how a ligament connects muscle to bone. Think about that: in the positive sense, religion is the deep bond that connects us to God and one another.

FAITH. Basically, *faith* means "trust." That, of course, immediately raises the question *"Who (or what) do you trust?"* In prison, the basic answer to that question is *"Nobody,"* at least nobody around you. The question about who's trustworthy, who's believable, who's faithful, is at the core of spiritual survival. In fact, it's at the heart of what it means to be a human being.

SPIRITUAL. This word seems to be everywhere these days. It's hard to define because people use it in all kinds of different ways. Sometimes it means "mysterious, not easily explained." Sometimes it means "not physical, not something you can put under a microscope." Sometimes it means "how I feel about things." The Bible takes a slightly different approach: the word *spirit* is used to describe how God is active, as "breath, wind, power, guidance, and creative force."

PRAYER. We're going to say more about prayer later on, but for now think about prayer as conversation with God. From our side of the conversation, it can be helpful to think of Christian prayer as coming down to four words:

> *Thanks!*
> *Sorry!*
> *Help!*
> *Wow!*

If you're having trouble knowing how to simply talk to God, then you might want to try starting with each of those words and seeing where it takes you.

> *"God, thanks for ...*
> *And I'm sorry that ...*
> *Please help by ...*
> *Wow! You're amazing because ... "*

SIN. *Sin* is a tricky word because it covers a huge range of things, and because it makes us uncomfortable. Basically, from a Christian point of view, *sin* describes everything that separates us from God. *Sin* can describe specific actions, but it can also be a quality of how we are. It can describe both the bad things we've done and the good things we've failed to do.

REPENTANCE. This doesn't mean thinking of yourself as a worm, or as unworthy of God's love. It means turning around, doing an about-face, and having a fundamental change of mind and heart.

HOLY. Sometimes, when applied to people we know, this word can have a negative connotation, as in "She thinks she's so holy! As if she's perfect!" But, biblically speaking, God's call for us to "be holy" isn't something that sets us *above* other people. It's God setting us *alongside* and *apart* for a special purpose. When we say that God wants us to be holy, we're saying that God has wonderful plans and purposes for our lives.

ETHICAL/MORAL. These two related words have to do with answering the questions, "How should we live? What would God have us do? Given that God loves me, what's the right response on my part?"

DISCIPLE. This is a kind of biblical, churchy word that basically means to be a learner, student or follower. One writer describes the practice of discipleship as a "long obedience in the same direction." For Christians, the one we learn from, the one we follow, apprentice ourselves to, and obey is Jesus.

Think About It. Talk About It.

1. What has your own experience of reading the Bible been like?
   a) life-changing
   b) confusing
   c) boring
   d) fascinating
   e) mixed—encouraging and inspiring but also frustrating
   f) to be honest, I'm not much of a reader
   g) I've never actually tried to read it

2. What do you think of the idea that the Bible is more like a big love story than a long list of rules and regulations?

3. Do you find it helpful to think about a variety of ways to read the Bible? Which of the six different suggestions do you find most appealing right now?

4. What other "spiritual" words do you think could use some explaining?

3

FORGIVENESS

I generally do believe that people want to be forgiving, but they aren't; they only want to appear to be. This is not a forgiving society we live in.
    —Nathaniel

I truly believe that all of us have some type of addiction within us.
    —James

It hurts to look in the mirror and see the person who destroyed my future.
    —Doaikah

I'm my biggest critic, but to overcome it you can't take yourself too seriously. I have to live with all my wrong decisions and bathe my mind in all the "what ifs." It eats at me.
    —Jose

I have never, not once, ever, seen the street life (gangs, crime, drugs) pay off for anyone. Try prayer, honesty. Be yourself. People respect a person who is just being himself. It's okay to have shortcomings—everyone does!
    —Dan

I struggle with totally surrendering myself to God. I am still holding on to things I know I should let go of.
    —Dennis

Let's face it. Real forgiveness is incredibly tough. It's tough for us. And it's tough for God, too. The author Lewis Smedes calls forgiveness "love's toughest work and love's biggest risk." We've learned that if we're going to find freedom, or to have relationships of any kind, then one way or another we're going to have to deal with the issue of forgiveness. And we've also learned that real forgiveness is not only tough, it's complicated. There are all kinds of angles to forgiveness. And so we asked a large group of inmates:

> Where do you personally struggle the most with forgiveness? Is it with forgiving others? With being forgiven by others? With accepting being forgiven by God? With forgiving God when you're mad at him? With forgiving yourself?

How about you? How would you answer? As you think about that, listen to what some of them had to say . . .

Forgiving others . . . seems so easy to do when I'm in prayer. But then afterward I find myself constantly going back to the trespass I feel someone has done to me. The exception to that is when someone apologizes and asks me to forgive them. Then it's easy. I don't know why that is.
—Kentes

Not being forgiven by others really does bother me. When someone has his heart hardened it seems like an impossibility to be forgiven by him or her.
—Anonymous

Forgiving others in jail is hard because they do the same thing all over again the next day! Half the time when someone says that they forgive me I don't believe them.
—Rodney

Love's Toughest Work

Real forgiveness comes into play when we've been hurt—personally, unfairly, and deeply. Real forgiveness is tough because, first of all, it's *unfair*. It's tough because it's *personal*. Here's what we've discovered about ourselves: we can think and say all kinds of things about forgiveness, but when it comes to actually forgiving the people who have personally hurt us—cheated us, wronged us, abandoned us, injured us—our instinct is either

(a) to strike back, or

(b) to stand at a distance with clenched teeth and crossed arms until the person who wronged us has paid for what they did. Every last bit. *They owe me!*

Love wants to do its tough work: forgiveness. But forgiveness is tough because we still feel hate. It's tough because we still hurt. It's tough because when we look at (or think about) the person who did us wrong, we don't see a person any more. We only see "the perpetrator." It's tough because our thoughts and our emotions are locked in the past, in a painful moment of time. Forgiveness is tough because it blesses and comforts the person who needs our forgiveness, and every instinct tells us not to open our hands in blessing, not to open our mouths with words of comfort.

Forgiveness is also *risky*. It's risky because even with loving forgiveness there are no guarantees. The person we forgive may, or may not, accept our forgiveness. They may accept our forgiveness and then continue to cause us the same hurt. They may even interpret our forgiveness as permission to keep hurting us. We may ask others to forgive us and they may not be able to. No guarantees.

But there's another side to forgiveness—the wonderful, freeing side. Because forgiveness is simply love in action. Because nothing feels better than forgiveness. There's nothing quite like feeling the weight of our guilt slip away. Nothing is more joyful than a fresh start with someone.

> Knowing that forgiving is not excusing makes real forgiveness possible.
> —Dan

Before we dig deeper into the heart and art of forgiveness, let's try to make things a little clearer by pointing out lots of things that forgiving is not.

First, forgiving is not trivial. We're not called to forgive every little mistake, every annoyance or disturbance, every minor slight or disappointment that we've ever received. True forgiveness is for the serious, deep and unfair hurt that we receive.

Second, forgiving is not excusing. In fact, excusing is the opposite of forgiving. If the person who hurt us was not to blame, if there were circumstances completely beyond their control, then forgiving is unnecessary and inappropriate.

Third, forgiving is not accepting. Forgiving is not overlooking and ignoring a little mistake by an otherwise wonderful person. Forgiving is dealing directly with the bad things they did to us.

Fourth, forgiving is not the same as tolerating or minimizing the bad things people do. When we tell people, "That's okay—no problem," we're not forgiving them. Forgiving involves holding someone accountable. Forgiving includes telling the truth that lying, betrayal, or brutality is unacceptable and intolerable, and that we will not be a doormat.

Fifth, forgiving is not weakness. Lots of us struggle with this. It requires incredible courage to confront someone else and to tell the truth in love—and then to let go of the desire for payback. It takes no strength at all for us to nurse a grudge.

The Heart and Art of Forgiveness

Forgiveness, at its heart, comes down to two words: *taking away*.

The biblical word for forgiveness literally means "taking away," "bearing away," "removing." Above all, forgiveness is used to describe what God takes away, bears away, and removes *from us*. And so, if we want to know what we're called to do in the tough work of forgiveness, we need to see how God forgives by "taking away."

The Bible says that God disconnects the wrong we've done from who we are. He separates and peels off our sins from our person. He takes it away and sends it packing so that he can see us in a whole new light.

Where does all this wrong and sin go? It gets nailed to Jesus Christ's cross. And when it goes there, the Bible tells us, it goes straight to the very heart of God. Like a desert absorbs the rain, our sin is totally absorbed deep down in the fire of God's overwhelming love—never to come circling back at us, defining us, accusing us, or convicting us ever again.

Forgiveness is God's new creation, a new way of seeing and a new way of being. The heart of forgiveness is God absorbing our hatred and lies and selfishness without ever retaliating. The heart of forgiveness is God's white-hot love for us.

We believe that Jesus calls us to a life of radical love, to a life of forgiveness, to love's toughest work and biggest risk. Jesus calls us to love our enemies, to forgive when we've been hurt unfairly and deeply—to forgive even when what we feel is hate. Jesus calls us to a new way of seeing other people—taking the sin away from the sinner who wronged us.

Jesus commands us to love and forgive our enemies even when it's really hard, even when the enemy is faceless or invisible, or when the enemy is our own regret.

But Jesus doesn't leave us on our own, sitting in our cells, full of hurt and hate, and now commanded to do something we just can't do. Jesus also gives us his Holy Spirit—God's own force who comes to us to encourage us and empower us to take the next step in the art of forgiving.

That's what forgiving is—an art, a combination of a gift we receive from the Spirit of Christ and a skill we acquire by actually doing it. Here are a couple of quick guidelines to get you going in the art of forgiveness:

1. *Pace yourself.* Don't rush it. Stop and think about what's bothering you. Maybe it's something that can easily be excused. Maybe it's something that you need to be forgiven for. Take some time to pray about it. Pace yourself. And yet . . .

2. *Don't wait too long.* Forgiveness is an urgent matter. In fact, Jesus told people to stop what they were doing, even right in the middle of worship, and go immediately to make things right. Jesus teaches us to make the first move. Don't drag your feet. Why? Because bitterness will inevitably set in, and your hatred will take root in your heart. Because death may intervene. Because it will only get harder to forgive in the future. Because the longer you leave it, the more your offer of forgiveness will sound and feel more like a bitter dredging up of bad things from the past than an opportunity for a new future.

3. *Forgive as often as you need to.* One of the toughest things about forgiveness—and in this way it's similar to grief—is that you're not always sure you've completely done it. Sometimes little things can trigger the old feelings of hurt and hate all over again. Those old wounds, those feelings of contempt, and the desire for revenge can just bubble up to the surface. And then you need to forgive again. Forgiveness is sometimes not so much a one-time act as it is an ongoing, mysterious process.

4. Keep putting the relationship first. In our desire for justice and revenge we tend to put rules first. And the rules say, "Behave this way and you're out. Cross this line, and don't bother coming back. Treat me this way, and you're no friend of mine, no brother of mine, no son of mine." But that's not the way of Jesus. He calls us to put relationships first.

5. Look for God's hand in the process. All along we've been saying that in forgiveness we don't sugarcoat the truth. And the truth is, we do some terrible things to each other. And yet in God's amazing mercy, we can also see God's hand reaching down to bring something good out of this difficult experience. In the midst of relationship bitterness, there's nothing sweeter than the taste of forgiveness.

Forgiveness. It's love's toughest work. It's love with its sleeves rolled up.

But we know about love. Love bears all things, believes all things, hopes all things, endures all things. Love never ends! (Be sure to check out the famous description of Christian love in 1 Corinthians 13.)

When It's Really Hard to Forgive

We can list all kinds of things we are called upon to forgive. And all of them are awful. *All* of them. The truth is, there's no top ten list of the worst hurts. How could we ever measure or compare such things? How can we ever truly know the depth of hurt or hate inside someone else? We don't even understand our own hearts all that well.

And yet, there are times when it's really, really hard for any of us to forgive, even when we want to forgive, even when our hearts are willing to forgive.

Jesus says, "Love your enemies," and forgiveness is part of what Jesus means by that. Forgiveness happens best when it can be eye-to-eye, face-to-face. But sometimes that just isn't possible because the person we need to forgive is gone.

Sometimes they avoid us. Other times the people we need to forgive are invisible. The unknown rival gang member who killed our friend— invisible. The bully who made school a living hell—long gone. And sometimes the people we need to forgive are already dead. They've died before we had a chance to face them and forgive them.

For some of us, the toughest work of forgiveness isn't the faceless enemy. More often than not, our biggest enemy has a face we know all too well. It's the face that we see in the mirror every morning.

Truth be told, many of us have a terrible time forgiving ourselves. Listen to what some of our guys said about this:

> I think of my childhood and of all the bad things I did as a kid: stealing from my family, lying to my mother, treating animals badly. Even though I was just a kid, I still can't find a way to forgive my childhood.
> —Wilfredo

> Once you own responsibility for your actions and begin on the road of repentance and redemption, God brings things back to your mind: shame, embarrassment, secrets you may have forgotten about, things you didn't ever want to remember, or those things you vowed to take to the grave with you. There's so much to deal with (and forgive yourself for) . . . and it's a process.
> —Anthony

> I think about the potential I had to live a successful life, and then become upset with myself all over again because I know that it's by my own actions that I am imprisoned. It hurts to look in the mirror and see the person who destroyed my future.
> —Doaikah

Why is forgiving ourselves so incredibly difficult for so many of us? Why does love's toughest work get even tougher when we're the cause of our own hurt?

> This has been and continues to to be a real sticking point. —Dan

Maybe one reason is because many of us don't trust ourselves—and for good reason. We know how easy it is for us to justify and excuse ourselves. We know how easily and how often we sweep the rotten things we do under the carpet. And so we don't trust an "inner judge" who says, "I forgive you. Smile, God loves you!"

That just seems too easy, doesn't it? And too phony. We find it hard to forgive ourselves because, as a general rule, most of us don't like *self-forgivers*. And so instead we choose an inner judge who we think is more just, but who never lets us off the hook. We walk around with an inner judge hounding us with all the bad things we've done. This judge peeks out at us from the mirror, reminding us of the rotten things we did to other people, telling us that we're worthless and unforgivable.

On the other hand, some of us find it hard to forgive ourselves because we're proud. Simple as that! We can't find it in ourselves to forgive ourselves because we can't really accept the fact that we aren't perfect! *"I, of all people, shouldn't have done that awful thing!"* In our pride we find it hard to accept the fact that we're as bad as everybody else and that we need forgiveness too.

In the end, lots of us find it really hard to forgive ourselves because we stop at regret. Regret is like a tape playing deep inside us that keeps repeating, *"What did I do? What did I do?"*

You might think that regret is healthy. And in a way, it can be. But here's the thing: Regret can also be dangerous. In the Bible, the word literally means "thinking about again," "caring about again," "being anxious about again." Regret means seeing and feeling the bitter results of sin over and over and over again.

Regret actually short-circuits the process of real forgiveness. We talked earlier about how the heart of forgiveness is God's permanent "taking away" and sending away of our sin from us. That means that failing to forgive ourselves is putting our sin back in orbit around ourselves so that it can continue to accuse us. And that's exactly what regret does. Regret is us telling ourselves that we are the enemy that can't be forgiven. Not fully. *Regret is "putting back" what God has "taken away."*

We need to stop regretting and start *repenting*. The Bible describes repentance as "godly sorrow," a practical turnaround of heart and mind that leaves no regret. "Godly sorrow brings repentance that leads to salvation and leaves no regret, but worldly sorrow brings death" (2 Corinthians 7:10).

No regret. How about that as a motto for Christian living! The Bible tells us that it's not our business to be judging ourselves or others any more, that it's not our business to hurl sins back in orbit around them or around ourselves. That's why the apostle Paul could say, "I don't even judge myself" (1 Corinthians 4:3) and "If God is for us, who can be against us?" (Romans 8:31). If God forgives us, who are we to undo what he has already done?

Finally, for some of us, the toughest act of forgiveness is when the enemy seems to be God himself. The truth is, most of us don't want to think of God as our "enemy." We know he isn't. That said, there can be those times when God feels like our enemy, when we feel unfairly hurt, and we know that God (somehow, some way) is in control and has something to do with this.

Sometimes, like Job in the Bible, we just want to come right out and say it:

> God, does it please you to oppress me? Do you get a kick out of it? Why did you bring me out of the womb? Just to crush me for no reason? I'm sick of the way you treat me. (Job 10)

Sometimes, like Jesus himself, we want to cry out, "My God! My God! Why have you forsaken me?" (Mark 15:34). *Why did you abandon me? Why did you leave me hanging? I thought we were friends, and now you treat me like we're enemies!*

It's hard to forgive God. It's hard to even know how to start. We're torn.

On the one hand, God is the one we're really mad at and disappointed with. But, on the other hand, God is the only one we can appeal to for help. We're torn between our gratitude and love for all that God's given us, and our anger at all that he's allowed to be inflicted upon us. It just doesn't seem right.

What do we do when our head says "I have no right to judge God!" and yet our heart feels the need to tell God how angry and disappointed we are? The Bible gives us some clues.

First, be honest with God. Don't try to fake it. Take it to God. He's big enough to handle it.

Second, be persistent. Commit your spirit into his hands. Continue to seek his face. Wait for that face-to-face encounter to come. Like Job, God won't keep us waiting forever. Like Job, a fresh start lies ahead. (Check out Job 38-42.)

Think About It. Talk About It.

1. Where do you personally struggle the most with forgiveness: With forgiving others? With being forgiven by others? With accepting being forgiven by God? With forgiving God when you're mad at him? With forgiving yourself?

2. What do you think about the biblical idea that the heart of forgiveness is God "taking away" our wrong-doing from us and absorbing it into himself?

3. Where do you usually tend to go wrong when it come to the art of forgiveness?
   a) I rush it.
   b) I wait too long.
   c) I find it hard to keep forgiving.
   d) I forget to make the relationship a priority.
   e) I forget that God's actively involved in the process.

4. Do you tend to suffer from bitter and recurring regret instead of repenting, accepting God's forgiveness, and moving on?

4

SHAME

Shame is different.

That's something we missed in our diagnosis of what's wrong with us in the first edition. Guilt and shame often go together, but they're not the same thing. Shame is a different experience, a different kind of feeling and thinking, a different kind of brokenness, a different kind of wound that needs a different kind of healing.

Shame makes us feel deeply flawed, inadequate, inferior, incompetent, unwanted, unliked, unacceptable. Shame can make us feel disgusted with ourselves. It can make us feel anxious around others—worried that we'll be found out and found wanting, that our dirty secrets will be exposed for the whole world to see. Shame makes us feel isolated and rejected and alone, like a disgraceful outsider who doesn't belong and who will never belong. Shame feels like a darkness that we carry around deep inside, like an emotional black hole that sucks up the light, like a smothering heaviness on our spirit, like a deeply buried anchor on our soul, saying, "Never forget how worthless, how not-good-enough, how unwanted you are. No one would want to be with you if they knew the real you." Shame can make us feel all of that, and at the deepest possible level.

But shame is more than just a feeling. It's also a mutually reinforcing set of beliefs and messages telling us we deserve to feel shame, telling us we really are unworthy, unwanted, unclean, and unacceptable. Some of us *believed* that we were unacceptable, and then we came to *feel* that way, which only made us believe it even more. And some of us first felt (or were made to feel) ashamed and unacceptable, and then we came around to believing it over time. Either way, it's a vicious cycle. Either way, it's hard to break free. And so most of us just try to cope the best we can, on our own, because shame tends to drives a wedge between us and others and between us and God.

Most of us end up using what researcher Donald Nathanson called the "compass of shame": four main strategies for coping with our shame. In a way, they line up with our primal responses to threatening situations: fight, flight, or freeze. So, for example, one way of coping with our shame would be to attack ourselves—beat up on ourselves, be habitually disgusted with ourselves. Another way would be to attack others—lash out in anger, shame them down to our level or below, so we don't have to feel so bad about ourselves by comparison. Those are the fighting responses.

But those are only two points of the shame compass. More often than not, we cope by going in other directions. Usually, our first response is to hide from others—to isolate ourselves, to cut others off, or, at the very least, to cover up and pretend. This is as old as Adam and Eve, who tried to hide from God (Genesis 3). But there's another way of hiding: hiding our shame from ourselves. We try to repress our shameful side, block it out, tamp it all down. We may distract ourselves with busyness or numb ourselves with addictive substances.

How many of us are locked up mainly because of how we've been coping with our shame?

Way too many of us are burdened by our toxic, chronic, secret shame. It's miserable. It's painful. And if you look, you can see it in the eyes of just about everyone in prison. Most of us have been bottling our shame up, stuffing it down inside. We continue to carry it around with us. Shame clings to those of us who tend to always compare ourselves to others (physically, socially, whatever) and who inevitably come up short. It hounds those of us who feel that we don't deserve anything. And it haunts those of us who've done some truly awful things in our lives, and now feel marked for life by it.

Shame grieves the heart of God, because none of this is what we're meant for.

All we're really doing by attacking or hiding, of course, is managing our shame. We're never truly dealing with it. Shame is elusive and tricky. It hides deep down inside. Shame has its own unique pathology. It's deeper and more global and more crippling than guilt. With guilt, generally, there's a way to confess for what we've done—to repent, make amends, and try to repair the relationship. But with shame, there's always the sense that if the other person knew who we really are (with all the mess deep inside us) they'd want out of the relationship altogether, because we're not worthy of forgiveness or love. We're stuck. Alone.

Shame is deeper than guilt, and it's more persistent than embarrassment.

Embarrassment is uncomfortable, but it comes and goes. It's episodic. We make mistakes. We all do painfully embarrassing things. The difference is, we can usually laugh about embarrassing moments later. But we don't laugh about truly shameful things, do we? Shameful pain lingers. It not only lingers, it grows. It becomes a chronic condition for many of us. It's like it seeps into our very way of being, percolating and staining everything about ourselves. It colors our every experience. It shapes our identity. It restricts our freedom. And it blocks us from God's love.

Who Are We, Really?

Shame has a way of touching the very core of our identity. It makes us ask ourselves, Who am I, deep down? What does all this inner dirt, stain, behavior, or thought say about me? What kind of person does the things that I do?

If we don't get this part right, these nagging questions about who we really are, we're going to keep getting shame wrong. Shame's going to keep weighing us down, and we'll never live the new and joyful life that Jesus calls us to.

There are two ways to get this question of identity really wrong, and one way to get it right.

Here's the first way we get identity wrong: Lots of us go wrong by making a fundamentally wrong equation. The author Lewis Smedes puts it this way: "I did, therefore I am; this is the fatal equation." It's saying that whatever stupid or awful thing I've done equals who I am. And we take that fatal, distorted, and overly simplistic equation and turn to Scripture, and guess what? There are plenty of biblical texts that seem to support it. In fact, Jesus' own language, about us being known by our "fruits" (good trees don't bear bad fruit; see Matthew 7:15-20), can just seem to pile on the shame.

Whenever we start making this on-to-one correspondence between fruit and root, this fusion between whatever bad thing I do and who I am, it's hard to avoid the defining power of all the bad fruit we've produced. It's hard to escape the moral logic that when I've done something awful and unacceptable, therefore I am something awful and unacceptable. Why?

Because . . . I did it. And I (not someone else) keep doing it. This is the fatal equation that keeps so many of us bound in our secret shame.

Here's the second way we get our identity wrong: We're tempted to reject the whole premise of shame altogether. We say, "Who I am inside has nothing to do with what I do on the outside." This way of seeing ourselves actually separates our being from our doing. So, we can say, "Yeah, I'm doing all these things, but you know, it really doesn't matter, because it doesn't really touch who I am on the inside. I am who I am, and I do what I do, and shame has nothing to do with it."

Here's the problem. If the first way of understanding who we are leaves us feeling perpetually shame-bound, this way leaves us shame-less. It also leaves us without a functioning conscience, disconnected from ourselves, lacking in integrity, and operating with a false self. Jesus has a word for us when we go this route, too: Hypocrite!

The good news is, there's actually a better way than either of these. There's a deeper, more honest, more profound, more hopeful, and more healthy way to understand our identity. There's a biblical way, a both-and way: We have both an old self and a new self. Dwelling in us are both sin and the power of the Holy Spirit. We have both an outer nature and an inner nature. We're both slaves to sin and part of the body of Christ.

You can't get more both-and than the famous passage in St. Paul's letter to the Romans.

> I need something more! For if I know the law but still can't keep it, and if the power of sin within me keeps sabotaging my best intentions, I obviously need help! I realize that I don't have what it takes. I can will it, but I can't do it. I decide to do good, but I don't really do it; I decide not to do bad, but then I do it anyway. My decisions, such as they are, don't result in actions. Something

has gone wrong deep within me and gets the better of me every time. It happens so regularly that it's predictable. The moment I decide to do good, sin is there to trip me up. I truly delight in God's commands, but it's pretty obvious that not all of me joins in that delight. Parts of me covertly rebel, and just when I least expect it, they take charge.

I've tried everything and nothing helps. I'm at the end of my rope. Is there no one who can do anything for me? Isn't that the real question? The answer, thank God, is that Jesus Christ can and does. He acted to set things right in this life of contradictions where I want to serve God with all my heart and mind, but am pulled by the influence of sin to do something totally different.— Romans 7:17-25, The Message

Paul knew that Jesus Christ can and does help us in the very midst of our shame. That's why Paul went on to say, "From now on, therefore, we regard no one from a human point of view. . . . So if anyone is in Christ, there is a new creation: everything old has passed away; see, everything has become new!" (2 Corinthians 5:16-17).

Are you putting these two pieces together? The Christian life is living with this double-self—the old self that's still kicking but passing away, and the new self, the Christ-shaped self, that's coming into being. And so all the shame that you and I still experience is the residue, the consequence, the ingrained patterns of our old self, the self that's on the way out. Our painful ongoing shame is associated with all of that. And it's real. But (and this is crucial) our sinful, shameful old self doesn't define our identity. Because there's something even more real about who we are and whose we are: our new life in Christ, the new creation, the rebirth, the abundant, free life in him.

Think About It. Talk About It.

1. What do you think about the idea that shame is different from guilt, and that the remedy for guilt is forgiveness and that the remedy for shame is acceptance? Do you find these ideas helpful?

2. Can you relate to the description of shame as a heavy feeling (and belief) of being fundamentally flawed, inadequate, inferior, incompetent, unwanted, unliked, or unacceptable? How real is that feeling in your life right now?

3. Shame most often begins at home. Looking back on your childhood, how consistently and effectively did your parents let you know that you were loved unconditionally? Did they consistently show pride and joy in you? Or did you get messages that made you feel inferior or unwanted?

4. Have you struggled with feeling or being "disowned" by parents? For those of you who are parents, how well do you think you're taking care of your children, showing pride in them, and taking joy in their existence? Do you think they feel shame?

5. The author Lewis Smedes lists people he calls "candidates for shame." These include people who are perfectionistic, overly responsible, morally scrupulous, compulsive comparers, approval addicts, never feeling deserving, condemned by bad memories, stuck in the shadow of a parent, or condemned by dreams. Do you recognize yourself in any of these descriptions? If so, how?

6. Which of the following have you used to cope with your shame?

a. *Attacking myself:* beating up on myself; having a chronic feeling of disappointment, even disgust, with myself

b. *Attacking others:* lashing out in anger, or shaming others to bring them down to my own level

c. *Hiding from others:* isolating myself, covering up my shameful side and pretending

d. *Hiding from myself:* repressing my shameful feelings, trying to distract myself with busyness or entertainment, numbing myself with drugs or alcohol

From Where I Sit: The Journey from Shame to Joy (Fred Nelson, Pastor)

Over the years, I've listened as AA members have come to me to do their fifth step and "admit the exact nature of their wrong." Every single person who's done that with me has had a story of dealing with a mountain of crippling unhealthy shame since childhood. Every single one.

There are all kinds of candidates for shame, and I'm one of them. We all have stories of where shame creeps into our lives. For me, shame came in childhood. It crept in through the door of growing up in an alcoholic family, and through the door of my own tendency to be a perfectionist.

My dad was an alcoholic, probably depressed, certainly secretly ashamed. And, as with many alcoholics, my dad's drinking led to all kinds of chaos and dysfunction for the rest of us. My sisters and brother all tried to cope with it, some by overeating, some by checking out, some by overachieving. I think my personality and ego led me to want to escape and overcome my family shame by being driven to be different and better.

I must've figured (sometimes consciously, mostly not) something like: The only thing I can do at this stage is to just work doubly hard at being good, and work doubly hard to be different from, better than, my family. In other words, overachieve my way into worthiness, into acceptance.

For as long as I can remember, I wanted to be, and expected to be, a "good kid"—an honest kid, a nice kid. I wanted people's approval and admiration. But at the same time, deep inside I felt like a terrible phony, pretending to be good but really just faking it. And I hated that about myself. Hated it.

It's horrible to live with the thought that, deep down, you're a fake. I lived that way for nearly forty years.

And then everything changed. For the past twenty years, my own personal reservoir of shame has been gradually draining away and giving way to joy. At the end of the day, I can only tell you what it's been like for me, my own path to God's joy. But maybe there's something in my story that'll resonate with yours.

For me, the path from shame to joy has been marked by four experiences and four key Bible passages. The first is an ongoing experience of God coming at me with grace and loving me and accepting me from the outside in. For years, I kept reading the gospel of Jesus Christ and repeating it to others. I'd tell people, "It's so obvious: God is crazy about you, don't you understand?"

As often as not, people would shrug, like they were afraid to believe it. "Yeah, okay. I guess so."

"No, I'm telling you. God loves you like crazy."

I never realized that shame was blocking them from hearing the truth about themselves. I found myself getting drawn back to St. Paul's letter to the Romans, where Paul says "God's love has been poured out into our hearts through the Holy Spirit, who has been given to us" (Romans 5:5). Not dribs and drabs. Poured. Drenched and overflowing.

I talked about God's love so many times to others that I finally started listening to it for myself. That means . . . God is crazy about me. Just because.

"Just because" meant that I didn't need to hide from God or impress him. His grace and acceptance just kept coming, just kept coming, just kept coming. Regardless. Relentless. God's "just because love" just plain wore down my shame. That's what grace does.

Shame lost its grip on me because the shameful voice in my head got drowned out by the voice of God's grace saying, I know who you are and what you've done. But hear this: I love you more than you can ever know. I love you more than you can ever know. And that love just piled up and piled up. Love just got poured in and poured in and poured in. And, over time, I found myself starting to love myself, "just because."

For me, at least, God's intervening love was the only power strong and persistent enough to break down my unhealthy shame, my secret self-disgust, and my drivenness to prove or earn my way to acceptance.

That made all the difference, but it was still only the first step. There were still obstacles to my joy. And that meant I had to learn the art of accepting myself.

I couldn't seem to shake a sort of lingering resentment against myself. I could let go of my resentments against other people. I did that all the time. That part seemed second nature somehow. Ah, but when it came to letting go of my self-resentment—not so much.

Let me tell you a story about what I think was going on. One gray November morning I had a summons to go to the Cook County Courthouse in Chicago to see if I had to serve on a jury. I went for the day because I had to. I'll be honest, I really didn't have the time or the inclination to be called to serve on a long trial. Or a short trial. So I was one happy guy when a bunch of us got a call over the loudspeakers saying, "Thank you, but the judge doesn't need your services today. You're free to go." And those of us waiting all thought, Yes! Thank you, Lord!

For me, that experience exactly mirrored what I needed to learn about forgiving myself. You see, for the longest time, I kept showing up day after day as my own judge and jury, rehearsing old accusations, hearing new ones, putting up feeble defenses, judging myself, and assessing appropriate punishment. It was exhausting. It was depressing. And, as it turned out, it was unnecessary. Because it was wrong.

And here's why: God's Word had been telling me all along, about as loudly as you can imagine, "Thank you, Fred, but the Judge doesn't need your services today." I heard God say that, but my unkind, unforgiving, ungracious little inner judge kept showing up for service anyway. I couldn't dismiss my inner judge until I meditated long and hard on something astounding that St. Paul said: "I do not even judge myself. . . . It is the Lord who judges me" (1 Corinthians 4:3-4).

Wow. Soak yourself in that verse. I did, and it changed me. For me it meant that I don't have to judge people, myself included. I don't have the inclination. I don't have the wisdom. I don't have the standing. It's just not my job. Period. And that means I'm free to go—no more boasting, no more blaming. No telling the real Judge how to do his job. I'm free to leave the inner courthouse in my mind and just get on with my life. Yes! Thank you, Lord!

It's hard to describe how freeing this is. It makes me want to share with anyone I can what it took me decades to say to myself with real conviction: Thank you, but the Judge doesn't need your services today. Or tomorrow, either. You're free to go, too.

Okay, third step, third experience, and third key biblical truth that made all the difference for me on my way from shame to joy. It was the combination, over time, of knowing (a) that I'm loved more than I'll ever know, (b) that I have nothing to prove or earn, (c) that I'm not the judge and that I'm free to get on with living. It was this trifecta of God's grace that finally just allowed me to relax.

Not relax in the sense of giving up or not trying anymore, but relax and be filled with the joy God had been wanting to give me all along.

Relax in the sense of accepting (gratefully) that the Lord is God and I'm not.

Relax in the sense that life is a huge gift and it's mine to enjoy.

Relax in the sense that I belong.

Relax in the sense that Paul meant it for me too when he said, "All things are yours . . . all are yours, and you belong to Christ, and Christ belongs to God" (1 Corinthians 3:21-23).

Soak yourself in that verse. This is what gives me an unshakeable foundation for the joy that I now feel. This is what keeps shame from creeping back in. Because I belong where it matters. I belong to the God who's breaking in everywhere with his "just because" love. Knowing that makes me grateful for what has been. And it makes me expectant for what will be. And now it's like God's gift of joy is sticking to everything the way that shame used to. Lightness now, instead of heaviness, whatever the circumstances.

The fourth and final experience of the ongoing healing of my own shame has to do with constantly claiming my identity—who I am, deep down. It has to do with me being honest and truthful about my old, shameful self and being hopeful and confident about my new, joyful self in Christ.

I remember reading how the great church reformer Martin Luther used to wake up each morning and tell himself, first thing, "I am baptized." Luther knew that he needed to be reminded, on a daily basis, who he was and whose he was. He needed to keep hearing that he belongs where it matters. I need to do the same thing—to reaffirm that "I am accepted." Here's why.

Although the beast, the voice, and the feeling of shame has quieted down for me, it's not gone. It lurks. It waits in hiding. It still gets in some zingers and tries to hook me back into the old way of living. For example, the voice of shame will say, "Fred, you're so weak!" And the voice of grace helps me say, "Yeah, that's right. You got me. I am weak. I'm as fragile as a cheap clay jar. But weak as I am, I'm also God's chosen vessel. Because I carry the treasure of the Holy Spirit inside this weakness. Because Christ wants to be with me and in me. And that makes all the difference. So shut up, shame."

And then the voice of shame will accuse me: "Fred, come on. Be honest. You don't have what it takes. You talk a great game, but you'll never keep it up." And the voice of grace helps me say, "That's right. It's true. I can't do this. Not on my own, I can't. But powerless as I am, I'm not alone. I have Christ. And I have others who'll pick me up and carry me when I need it. I don't have to—and I don't want to—do life on my own. Not anymore. I'm part of the body of Christ. And that makes all the difference. So, shut up, shame."

At that, the voice of shame usually retreats for a while—until my next major screw-up. And then it comes roaring back, with this knowing look, saying, "See! I knew it. Only a matter of time. You're just a life-long screw-up, a prodigal, and now a phony and hypocrite to boot! That's the real you! How dare you call yourself a child of God! And a pastor? Give me a break!"

The voice of God's grace is helping me to say, "That's right. I am a prodigal. And a rebel and a phony." And just like the prodigal son, I do find myself saying, "Father, I've sinned against heaven and against you. I am no longer worthy to be called your son. Treat me as something less."

But then I hear the voice of the Father himself, both ignoring and overriding everything I can possibly say about my own worthiness or unworthiness. And what the Father is saying is, "Bring out the best robe. Put on the ring. Fire up the stove. Because this son of mine is alive again. This son of mine is home again, right where he belongs. And now, it's party time. Just because."

"This son of mine!" You hear that, shame? In your face.

Wherever your own shame stories began, whatever twists they've taken, and whatever dark and painful roads they've led you down, know this: God's grace can and will redeem them all. God's grace, his just-because love, his bottomless joy and acceptance and pride in you—all of it—is in store for you. Not just for some of us. For all of us. You. And not just some day. Now. Shame is on its way out. And God's grace is on its way in. It's irresistible. And it's amazing. And it's for you.

As you read these words on your prison bunk, hear them loud and clear. They are meant for you, right here, right now: *You are accepted.*

Think About It. Talk About It.

1. We only shame ourselves by the lies and half-truths we tell ourselves. Some of these self-deceptions include things like

- downplaying our positives

- exaggerating our flaws

- insisting on judging ourselves by undefined or impossible ideals

- turning specific criticism of what we do into blanket judgments about who we are

- reading (projecting) our own shame onto other people's minds

Do you recognize any of those characteristics in yourself? If so, do you think you can be on the lookout for these shame-prone tendencies in the future?

2. Which of the following sources of shame have been the strongest in your life?

a. My family—they never gave me the love every kid deserves.

b. My peers—they made me feel weak, stupid or unwanted.

c. My church—they made me feel like I would never be good enough.

d. Our society—they make me compare myself to unattainable ideals.

e. My own thought process—I'm my own worst enemy by the way I keep shaming myself.

3. Discuss which of the following statements best lines up with how you understand yourself.

a. What I've done equals who I really am.

b. What I've done has nothing to do with the real me.

c. I have both an old sinful self and a new self in Christ within me.

4. What are you most struggling to accept deep down?

a. God is crazy about me and delights in me, just because.

b. I'm free to stop judging myself and just let God be the real judge of me and others.

c. I can relax in my own skin in every circumstance because I belong to Christ and Christ belongs to God.

d. I'm still every bit as acceptable to God even when I'm weak, rebellious, or hypocritical.

5

COMPLICATED STUFF

I went through a period of using drugs, up to the point of overdos-ing one night, only to find out that the people that I was shooting drugs with (the same people I thought were my friends) had rolled me up in a rug and robbed me and my home while I laid in the alley.
  —Nathaniel

When I was addicted to weed I couldn't live without it.
  —Duncan

I was addicted to the fast lifestyle, women and money. My sole purpose in life was to satisfy my desires to the fullest. I was addicted to self-gratification, and the need was so strong that I sacrificed my friends for it.
  —Dennis

Well, the devil led me to my addictions, presented them to me and I went for this destructive behavior.
  —Jacques

For the longest time coke and weed were constants for me: "I could go for a joint right now." For me it was more than a desire. It was integrated into my very personality and identity. It was who I was.
  —Melvin

You, Addiction, and God: Been There. Done That.

What's wrong with us? What's goes on inside us that leaves us so broken and conflicted, so at war with ourselves, and so seemingly unable to change? The more we wrestle with that question, the more we search inside ourselves, the more we get to know others, the more we listen deeply to God's word, the more we think the answer is that *we're addicted.*

We're not just "trespassers," line-crossers who cross over and then back again. We're addicts. We're fallen. Stuck. Broken. Enslaved. To use the Bible's language for it, we have *demons* we can't get rid of. We're afflicted and torn and broken. We're in bondage and in deep need of deliverance.

The Bible doesn't use the word *addiction.* But when it talks about sin, the Bible is talking about the very same awful reality. Replace the word "sin" with "addiction" in the Bible, and often you'll wind up with essentially the same result: "If we claim to have no sin [or "addiction"], we deceive ourselves, and the truth is not in us" (1 John 1:8).

What does it mean to say we're all *addicted?* What is addiction, anyway? Let's just start with a quick definition we ran across:

> Addiction is any compulsive, habitual behavior that limits the freedom of human desire. It is caused by the attachment, or nailing, of desire to specific objects.

Addiction is a behavior, something we do, actions we take. Thinking included. Addiction is what happens when our God-given, in-built desires—our capacity for joy, for loving God and loving others—gets attached to other things. Interestingly, the word *attached* literally means "nailed to." So, instead of our desires being met by God, they get diverted, hijacked and nailed to something else—all kinds of something else. Things, people, drugs, feelings, thought patterns, behaviors—the list is endless.

And it's not as if each of us struggles with only one or two things. Truth is, we usually have all kinds of addictions at any one time. The Bible says that one time Jesus encountered a man who was enslaved by demonic forces inside him. And when Jesus commanded the demons to show their true identity, they said, "Our name is Legion." Literally, they said, "There's thousands of us inside this one man." (Read Mark 5:1-20 for the full story.)

> It feels like addictions are the attempt to fill emptiness—plain and simple.
> -Dan

Addiction has some tell-tale signs.

Sign #1 is tolerance: *"If I could only get more, everything would be fine."*

Sign #2 is withdrawal symptoms: *"This really hurts."*

Sign #3 is mind tricks: We play them on ourselves, sabotaging ourselves so that we can keep doing the addictive behavior. The greatest mind trick is, *"I can handle it."*

Sign #4 is loss of willpower: If you're wondering if you're addicted to a behavior or not, try this little test. Go ahead and stop. *And stay stopped.* If you're successful, congratulations, you're not addicted. Otherwise, join the crowd.

Addiction is everywhere. It's so pervasive that we get addicted in every part of who we are—from our cells to our souls. Scientists tell us that it happens in our bodies, down to the level of our very cells, in our neurological wiring, in our brain chemistry. In response to repeated behavior or substances, our brain and our cells adapt. They form chemical attachments, and new wiring develops that never fully goes away. And although we may not act on a particular behavior for a long while, the wiring is all there—ready to fire up again at a moment's notice. Our brains never forget.

There's a fascinating biblical passage from St. Paul that connects with this. Paul wrote in a letter about being given what he called "a thorn in the flesh," and about how he asked God repeatedly for that thorn to be taken away. But it never was completely taken away. Instead, Paul said, God's answer to him was, "My grace is sufficient for you, for power is made perfect in weakness" (2 Corinthians 12:7-10). Though God's grace can and does meet us in our weakest places, on a physical level, at least, we're never entirely free. Some thorns won't ever go away.

We're not only addicted in our bodies. We're also addicted in our minds. And that's the biggest battleground of all. Addiction has a way of splitting our will in two: one part of us aching for freedom, the other part dedicated to continuing the addictive behavior. And so, when one part of us tries to be free, the mind games of the other part kick into gear.

One mind game is denying and repressing: *I don't have a problem.*

Another is rationalizing: *I deserve it. Life is short. At least I'm not like them.*

Another is hiding, first from ourselves and then from others. *It's just my little problem.*

The smarter we are the more we try to complicate things—as a way of delaying quitting: *I've just got to figure out a way to stop. Tomorrow! Just one more! Just as soon as . . .*

Sometimes we start saying *"I can't handle it"* as a sneaky way of giving in to it—as a way of saying, "Who cares, anyway?" But that's just another delaying tactic.

Eventually we start saying, *"I can handle it,"* as yet another mind trick to get us to try to "manage" things. We'll do anything to keep the addictive behavior going.

If all that weren't bad enough, much of this is happening subconsciously, out of sight. Most of the time, we don't even understand our own motivations. And even if we do, there's no half-way step. Both God's Word and bitter personal experience teach us that the more we try to moderate, to cut down or "manage," the deeper we get attached to our addictions. That just starts a downward spiral: The worse we rebound when we inevitably fail, the more we lose hope, the more we beat ourselves up, the more defective and worthless and unclean we feel, and the stronger our demons get.

One time Jesus talked about this terrible out-of-control spiral and about what happens when we try to clean our spiritual house ourselves and get free without God's grace. He said we might clear out that unclean spirit *for a while,* but it'll inevitably come back with a vengeance—bringing a whole bunch of even more evil spirits with it and leaving us worse off than when we started (Matthew 12:43-45). That's exactly what we experience when we try to handle and control our way out of addiction.

> In A.A. we talk about our alcoholic selves and our real or healthy selves—how our alcoholic selves use any means to destroy us.
> -Dan

We get addicted in our bodies, and our very own cells conspire to keep us addicted. We get addicted in our minds, and our very own minds play tricks on us. The apostle Paul talked about this internal agony and struggle: how we've lost our freedom; how we can't do the good we want; how we do the very things we don't want to do; how we're at war with ourselves—quite literally killing ourselves (Romans 7:14-25). Like us, the people Jesus freed from addiction and demonic forces were people in desperation. They were on the edge, out of their right minds, at risk, alienated, alone, out of control.

This is life and death. For some of us, and for our friends and family, this is *physical* life and death. For others, this is *psychological* life and death. We feel tortured and depressed by endless mind games and shattered self-esteem. And for all of us, this is *spiritual* life and death. Our addictions are tearing us in two, robbing us of our freedom, and disconnecting us, on a fundamental level, from God and from everyone else. Addiction not only sucks the life out of us, it sucks the love out of us.

No wonder St. Paul cried out in his letter, *"Wretched man that I am! Who will rescue me from this body of death?"* (Romans 7:24). But then he immediately answers his own question. Who will? God will, through Jesus.

We're at the heart of the mystery of addiction and salvation. The mystery of the things we know and the things we don't know. We know *who* (Jesus), but we don't know *how*. We know that Jesus was, and is, able to meet people in the midst of their bondage and deliver them—set them on the way to freedom. What we don't know is *how* those demons and addictions got broken. It takes both human faith and God's grace, but exactly how those two intersect—how our tiny mustard seed of faith can help set us free—that we don't know. What we do know is that Jesus healed where there was no human hope left. What we don't know is how God can love us that much.

Breaking the power of addiction always involves a painful process of detaching, of "un-nailing." Have you ever struggled to pull a nail out of a piece of wood? There's often a lot of resistance. It can leave some ugly scars. That's what it can feel like to un-nail ourselves from our addiction. Other times it can feel as if we're walking through a desert with a deep emptiness inside—hoping that God will somehow show up there with us.

What we don't always know is how to answer the awful underlying questions: What do we really want most? Do we want God for himself? Or do we want God only in order to get us out of our painful addiction? Do we truly want to be free for God and for others? Or do we still want to be free to pick and choose our addictions?

The way to the true freedom is going to take honesty, responsibility, simplicity, and patience. It takes honesty, because so much of what we do is deceptive or hidden. It takes responsibility, because God delivers us from our addictions so that we can finally live responsibly before him. It takes simplicity, because in the end it all comes down to quitting. The simplicity to just refuse to do it and keep on not doing it. The simplicity of not complicating things by substituting some other addiction.

Finally, it's going to take patience. Not infinite patience, but life-long patience. True freedom as an ongoing condition isn't available to us in this life. For now, our brains, our minds and our spirits will keep on attaching to inferior things. And yet God is always there, every step along the way, ready to help us detach—and giving us grace and power to reattach to him. Listen to how some addicted inmates talk about their addictions now.

I've learned that God can deliver me from anything, and that I can come to him the way I am and that he will change me.
—Volney

Well now the same thing (about my addiction) can be said about my faith in God: I can't live without him.
—Duncan

God has allowed me (through Christ) to change my desire from pleasing myself to pleasing him.
—Dennis

I'm so happy that my addiction is with the Lord now. I can honestly say that all I crave now is the truth and knowledge of my heavenly Father.
—James

The first thing you learn in A.A. is that you cannot overcome your addiction without having a "higher power." For me that higher power is God. When facing my addiction I needed to remain strong and not give in. Most importantly, faith in God gave me something to stay sober for!
—Doaikah

I asked God to take away my desire for alcohol and drugs, and since then I have felt free of my addictions.
—Robert

Through my faith in God (and much prayer) he has delivered me from returning to this destructive lifestyle.
—Jacques

It wasn't until I started getting a new mindset and a new identity through my faith in Jesus that the addiction lifted. I no longer saw myself and identified myself as a gang banger or a drug addict. I'm God's man now.
—Melvin

One day the fullness of freedom will be ours. But not yet. For now we wait and groan together. For now it will have to be enough to hear God's answer to each of us, "My grace is sufficient for you." God's grace is sufficient and amazing. And it's for you—God's man. Let the chains fall away.

Think About It. Talk About It.

1. Do you accept the idea that we're all addicted to something, that our God-given desires have become attached to the wrong things? Have you ever struggled with addiction?

2. What are your favorite mind-games to keep your own addictive behavior going (denial, rationalizing, hiding, complicating things, managing things)?

3. Do you truly want to be free for God and others? Or do you still want to be free to pick and choose your addictions?

4. Do you honestly believe that God is powerful enough to help you detach from your addictive behavior and begin to reattach to him?

From Where I Sit: You, the Gangs, and God; Various Inmates, Stateville Prison

We sat down with Melvin, a former gang boss in Chicago, to share his experiences and his thoughts about how the gang life and Christian life look to him now.

When we were young and aggressive we found ourselves running to the gangs, saying, "I'm here!" Most of us were fatherless kids. And that lack of father leaves a wound inside us. We had been told that we were "the man of the house." But we didn't know the first thing about what it meant to be a man. We were just looking for acceptance. We were empty on the inside and we tried to fill that emptiness with the street life.

I come from a functional family; though my father left our home, my mother took it upon herself to be our provider. But I was fascinated by the life of many around my neighborhood. I went to school and even graduated from high school and junior college. But the world was tugging at me real hard. I had great jobs, but my mom would say that I was a professional by day and a thug by night.

I got introduced to the Rasone Spanish Cobras and started bidding their work. Got involved in drugs, both using and selling. Made a lot of money, but something was missing in my life. I allowed myself to be prostituted by the devil's scheme, and now I find myself fifteen years incarcerated for a crime I'm innocent of. Just being part of something negative can drag you to the grave—or if you're lucky enough, into jail.

The tendency in here is like it is outside: to run to the gang saying, "I'm here!" I see it every day. And instead of taking a moment to gain some wisdom for once in your life, you find yourself talking some nonsense about what new snacks are in the commissary. You're going to walk onto the deck looking to get hooked up, because you fear the unexpected. You look around to see who you need to respect. Who's done the most time? Who can make something happen?

I was a gang boss on the outside. And then in here I was a Unit

Coordinator for years. When a new guy would come into our deck and wouldn't be hooked up with anyone, we'd go to "the box." The box would have toiletries, some food, little things that any inmate needs. We'd give him a bag with things he needed. That was a signal that he's ours, he's protected. A little while later we'd come and demand double the amount back. That's how it is with the gang.

Later, after I became a Christian, we began keeping our own box, too. Now, when a new guy comes onto the deck needing something, we go to the box and take him a bag. The difference is, we don't demand double in return. In fact, we don't even ask him to pay it back at all. We just tell him that God loves him and ask him to help out the next guy if he can. That's how it is with the Christians.

Before I became a Christian, I had all the benefits of being a gang chief, but something was missing. I grew up an anti-church guy in a Catholic family with a spiritist connection. I was converted during a song, sung by a singer at a faith service. To be honest, I had gone to pass messages to other inmates. But he sang "I'm so glad troubles don't last for always. Weeping may come for a night; don't worry, it'll be all right." That's when I realized God was missing in my life, that God was what I needed to fill that void in my life.

I left the gang when I reached the point that I knew I couldn't stay any more. I had a new life, and a new identity in Christ. So I went and told them I had to leave.

They knew me. They knew that I had integrity, and they could see that I didn't have any ulterior motives. They said, "Okay, but be sincere about it." They simply let me go. It surprised a lot of people.

For a while some of them couldn't understand why I left. Some of them called me a coward. Others took my leaving as a personal betrayal. But later they watched me in my new life and came to respect me. Some even followed me out of the gang.

When I meet a new inmate, I ask him, "If it's not too much to ask, how much time were you given?" If he's open to that, I would ask, "Are you hooked up (with a gang)?" If he was, I'd share my story with him.

"Let me share something with you," I'd tell him. "Regardless if you're innocent or guilty of what you've been accused of, know that there is hope. The gang has done nothing for me, even though I had a spot. The gang is not going to do anything for you, either. In jail, all they're going to do—if you allow them to—is to drag you into more trouble and even getting more time.

"I tell you all this just to say—you need to get your priorities straight if you want to survive in this place. Please don't allow someone to send you off on a mission. My brother, I'm not trying to tell you something I've not been through or seen. I'm just here to share a message of hope.

"Today, I stand for the greatest organization known to mankind, the Kingdom of God. Today, I'm a follower of Jesus Christ. Ever since I gave my life to the Lord, things have started to look brighter. My legal journey is starting to take form. Relationships that were scarred are now up and running. Even those who doubted my transformation are today convinced that serving the Lord is the right course of action in our lives.

"I'm not trying to force my belief in you, but I will tell you that the Word of God says, 'Apart from me you can do nothing' (John

15:5]. My brother, there is hope in the midst of it all. But it's up to you! 'God has a plan for you, a plan to prosper you and not to harm you, a plan to give you hope and a future' (Jeremiah 29:11]. It won't be an easy journey—I won't lie to you. But I can guarantee that if you start living the life God has for you, he will do the impossible for you and your family."

Then I would ask to pray for him and invite him to seek me whenever in need. I would reassure him that I wanted to help him. I would give him my information. And then I would leave it up to him and God.

Other former gang members talk about themselves, their gang experience, and God.

Jail is a rite of passage for some kids. They turn to gangs because they show them a lot of love. They've raised themselves and are pissed off at the world. A child does what a child wants to do. But I would remind him that God is real and this is definitely not the place he wants to end up. Let me tell you from personal experience, gangs are the fastest way to get a life sentence for something you may not have done.
    —Rodney

Look around. Your gang got you sent somewhere you don't want to be. Your first "to-do" should be to develop a relationship with Jesus Christ and experiencing the peace that he will give.
    —Duncan

Gangs are not the way of life—they won't be there when you need them most. They can't get you out of prison.
    —Kevin

I came in here at age 18 and I've been locked up for seventeen straight years. I was sentenced to two natural life sentences for two first-degree murders due to my involvement in a gang. I'm now an ex-member, but my choice as a teen cost me my freedom in the years of my youth. I've never been married. I have no kids. My family and friends and loved ones all left me to be alone. I have never had one visit at Stateville. Not one. Gangs aren't worth the risk of you never becoming what God has called you to be—a man of God. I still pray for a second chance. You may have one, so please don't let the gang (or anyone else) hinder your life or destroy your humanity. Get out and stay out!
    —JT

The truth is, gangs can't help you the way you want them to. They look for what you can do for them. And remember that God can do the impossible in your life.
    —Volney

Look around your cell. You've done it your way, and the gang's way. Do you think it might be time to give God a serious, whole-hearted try?
    —Kentes

The only gang you should ever have is "family and Christ." If you truly, truly want to feel what a true family can do for you, then just sit back for a while and watch what God can do to a man's life when he truly surrenders to Christ! He is the only one who will have our backs! And remember that we Christians will always be there for you if you ask. We've traveled that same lonely road of faith. God hasn't stopped loving us, so why would we ever stop loving you?
    —James

Everyone else may have turned their back on you, including the gang, but God never will. More than that, he wants to welcome you into his family so that he can bless you in ways you never could imagine.
    —Dennis

Like Melvin, Jacques spoke at length about gangs and God.

I was second seed to the top of leadership in one of the largest Latino street gangs in the city of Chicago. A lot of my life was spent on the streets, and it's a lifestyle. So, once I got here, my Lord knew that this is where he would get my attention. And believe me, he tried for many years!

He started by removing me out of the gang, and removing the gang lifestyle out of me. The first thing he told me was the "Parable of the Unjust Steward" (check out Luke 16) with the line, "No servant can serve two masters." In other words, I couldn't continue to serve the gang and him.

Both the Christians and the gangs emphasize unity and profess love. Gang love is not authentic, though. Christians reach out to people with love; gangs control people with debt. They won't suffer for you the way Christians will.

Let people know what happens when you join a gang, and we'll see how many people join then. Gangs prey on the young; nine times out of ten young people in the city are looking for someone to love them. Gangs teach young people to trust your gang and no one else. I greeted some new inmates, calling them "brothers"; neighboring gang leaders tried to stop me from calling them that. The gangs want to tell you who you can call brother.

I would tell a young man being tempted by gangs, "Let's move me, you, and gangs out of the way and move God to the front!" More than likely, that's the reason most of us are in prison in the first place: we are always putting someone or something before God in our lives.

The gang was my downfall. It's like being sick all the time and wanting to find out what's causing you to be sick—you want to know what the problem is. God showed me what the problem was all along. It's not too late! "Seek the Lord while he may be found, call on him while he is near" (Isaiah 55:6). God says, "I know the thoughts I think toward you . . . thoughts of peace and not of evil, to give you future and a hope" (Jeremiah 29:11).

Think About It. Talk About It.

1. Have you ever been involved with a gang? If not, why not? If so, what do you think you were looking for from the gang?

2. Jacques talks about how he was struck by Jesus saying that no man can serve two masters. For him that meant that you can't serve both God and the gang. Do you agree? Why?

3. Many of the guys talk about how the gang brought them more grief than good, and that it took more than it gave. Do you think that's true?

4. How do you think God feels about gangs?

5. Do you agree that it takes courage to be a Christian and say no to the gang? Who could support you in that move?

Maintaining (or Regaining) a Meaningful Relationship with Your Family

One of the earliest and best pieces of advice we got about this *Spiritual Survival Guide* came from an inmate named Dan.

What you might want to go further into is when a girlfriend or wife leaves. That happens *all* the time. Maybe abandonment or loneliness issues. All too often families pull away once the person has been sentenced.

When we shared an outline of this book with a group of inmates, their attention was immediately drawn to hearing what family members actually think and feel about maintaining a relationship with a family member who's in prison. "That's *deep*," they kept saying.

They were right. It *is* deep. And it's deeply personal. When it comes to family relationships, there's no one-size-fits-all description. There are all sorts of complicating factors. How good was the relationship before you got locked up? Has there been a long history of problems? How much damage has been inflicted on it recently? How good are you at sharing your thoughts and feelings with one another? How often do you see one another? How honest is everyone being with each other?

Every guy who's locked up has a different story to tell. There are those who have kept—and believe it or not, even improved—their relationships while in prison.

> My faith helps me maintain my relationship with my family because I'm an inspiration and encouragement to them. They hear me talk about God and the effects of prayer, and I believe that it inspires them to pray and attend church a little more. God helps me through my loneliness by providing me with other believers to have a relationship with.
> —Duncan

I've kept a good relationship with my parents. I believe that a belief in God is an essential part of life—especially human relationships. The "God part" allows me to stand back and see the bigger picture. When any of my relationships are strained I can remember that compared to the workings of the universe, it's just not that important. When I'm alone in my cell, I pray.
—Dan

My family has been by my side the whole time. For that I'm thankful to God for the support that I've received. I also have a loving Christian wife whom I share my thoughts and concerns with as well. We put God first in our marriage, then each other, and then ourselves.
—Robert

My family (mother, step-father, brothers, sisters, nieces, and nephews) weren't raised with any religion. So when I started reading the Bible, I noticed the love the Lord has for us and I started sharing with my family by showing them love. Some of our families weren't really raised with love!
—Wilfredo

Other guys have managed to keep (or in some cases, regain) a healthy relationship with their family, but they talk about struggling with loneliness.

I have always been able to maintain a good relationship with my family during my incarceration. But this relationship does not prevent me from feeling lonely. Although I do not feel really "abandoned," I feel that there are pieces missing in my life.

—Doaikah

My relationship with my wife and family has improved tremendously, because they see the change in me. But obviously, even though I've received Christ into my life, I still miss my wife and family, and I get lonely at times. When that happens, I pray and read the Bible and it renews my faith and hope.

—Dennis

I finally know how to truly love and appreciate my family. It's true, I still feel loneliness. But in the middle of that, God's promises encourage me: "I will never leave you or forsake you or leave you an orphan. Even if your own father and mother forsake you, I am there." This really encourages me.

—JT

I admit, this place is as lonely a place as a man could be in. I truly miss my family and friends, but God always intervenes, and I feel the love he has for me through memories, through the Holy Spirit, and (believe it or not) sometimes through the pain I endure.

—Coulter

Finally, a large number of inmates struggle as they think about the family relationships they never had, or have lost along the way.

I have not regained my relationship with my family yet. However, God has helped me through my loneliness by giving me Christians here in prisons as brothers, and by giving me pen pals to write to on the outside.
—Kevin

I have faith. But I don't have a relationship with my family. When I got locked up they turned their back. But I still love them. Because God didn't turn his back on me, I don't feel abandonment and loneliness in the same way.
—Timothy

My family loves me but half of them never visit or write, so that tells me how much they really care.
—Rodney

I've actually never really known anything but my immediate family, and that in itself is a very strained relationship. I've learned not to feel abandoned, because I know that God loves me.
—Nathaniel

I don't really have too much contact with my family. I do get to talk to my mom every Sunday. I think that my faith helps reassure her that I am in God's good hands now.
—Jacques

Some relationships appear to be irredeemable for you— and only God and time can heal that wound. God's helped me deal with my loneliness and feeling of abandonment by helping me get outside of myself. I've made an effort to make amends with those I miss. I've learned not to dwell or have too much self pity.
—Anthony

One way or another, your arrest and incarceration (and whatever led up to it) has had an impact on your family. It has created all kinds of turmoil—emotional, psychological, financial, spiritual. It may have come as a sudden shock, or it may have come as one more thing in a long series of dealing with you. Either way, your family has been through a lot.

We went and talked to some family members who have a son or husband or father in prison. We asked them about the range of feelings that they were going through. Not every family member feels exactly the same way, of course, but there was a surprising overlap in what they told us.

Your family has been through a certain amount of *shame and guilt*. Shame, because they sometimes don't want to show their face around other people. They're tired of being known as "the parent whose son is in prison." Sometimes they just want to hide from that. On another level, many family members carry around a certain amount of guilt. In their dark moments, they beat themselves up for not being a good enough parent. They torture themselves with whether they did the right things.

Sometimes they feel *depressed* to the point of being *physically sick*. Mothers, especially, are hurting, because they know that their sons are hurting. You know how you feel helpless dealing with the legal and prison system, right? Well, so does your family. They've been bounced around, been given conflicting information, and waited through endless court hearings. They're sick of it all.

They've been dealing with *fear* for a long time. And they still are. There was the fear of what you were getting yourself into. There was the fear of what the next phone call in the middle of the night might mean. There was the fear of the night you first got arrested. There was the fear of what would happen to you in lock-up. Then there was the fear of how your case would turn out. Now there's the fear of what will happen to you behind bars, whether you'll come out a hardened criminal—or at all. Some mothers have a terrible fear of dying while you're in prison and worry about what that will do to you. At some level they're afraid of the day you do get out—they're afraid you'll start the craziness all over again.

And so they feel *anxious*. A lot. What are you going to say in your next letter? Is there going to be a next letter? On one level, it's a huge relief to some of them now that you're locked up. At least they know where you are. They're not as worried that the next phone call will be the police, or the psych ward, or the morgue—or you, asking them to bail you out of a jam again.

They're *drained*. Emotionally spent. And sometimes, financially drained as well. The path that leads to prison puts a huge dent in a lot of families' finances. They don't have much left in the emotional bank, either. They've been caring for so long that there's no longer much positive emotion left. And so when you call demanding, "Help me! Take care of me now!" they're thinking, "Oh, now he wants help! How many times before did we offer and he refused?"

From time to time they find themselves *really, really angry*. Mom's so angry with you that she could just hit you across the head. Hard. And then they're angry with themselves for losing control and saying so many nasty things. At some level they feel betrayed, angry at God. *Why my kid? What did I do to deserve this, God?* They're often angry at each other. They're still hurling accusations at each other. *Why weren't you a better father? Why did you baby him? Why do you keep enabling his addiction?*

From time to time they feel *beaten down, robbed of a son, numb* and *just plain tired*. Sometimes they feel like they need to put on a show when they write or come to visit you. They like seeing the sober you, but they feel they need to put on a show for you. They're not sure if they should hide the good things from you (will that depress you?) or the bad things (will that depress you even more, since you can't do anything about it?).

Your particular family may not have been through all of this, but they've been through a lot. And what many of them need right now is time to decompress, to be free from your chaos, to heal a bit. And that's tough on you, because the timing couldn't be worse! Just when you're finally ready to reach out to them and have a healthy relationship, they find that they need to pull back from you to heal and protect themselves for a while.

Maybe the number one spiritual challenge facing you when it comes to your family is putting you and your needs to the side and putting their needs first. When you're locked up, the natural tendency is to become even more focused on yourself. And this can be a good and healthy process for you. It's a good thing to look inside yourself. It's a great thing to focus on your relationship with God.

But at the same time, you can become so self-absorbed that you forget the needs of other people. You can act like it's "all about you." And truth be told, your family may have had enough of you for a while.

What would God have us do about this period of time while we're feeling extremely needy and our family is feeling the need to heal from the wounds we inflicted on them? How can we love our family members during this time in practical ways, and hopefully grow those relationships? Here are a few suggestions.

1. *Pray for your family.* Remember, it's not all about you. Set aside what you need for the moment (don't worry, God's got your back) and focus on them. Pray for them to heal emotionally. Pray that they might survive and manage financially. Pray that they might get along with each other. Pray that they might have strong faith in the Lord. Pray that they might make it through whatever struggles they might be facing. Don't forget to thank God for every one of them.

2. *Ask God to give you patience.* Many people who are locked up have

trouble being patient. We're impulsive and demanding. Ask God to change that part of you. Ask for help in not forcing issues with your family. Give people the time that they need. Don't force people to follow your sense of urgency.

3. *Ask God for help with understanding and forgiveness.* This is a process, so be patient with yourself. Work on truly forgiving the father you never knew, or who abandoned you. Work on forgiving your family when they instinctively pull away from you. Forgive them when they let you down. And on the other side of forgiveness, apologize individually to people that you may have harmed. Don't make excuses for yourself—simply admit your fault and then ask for (don't demand) forgiveness.

4. *Ask God to help you let go of things you can't control.* You already know that you don't have control of things inside prison, right? So why try to control what's happening on the outside? Ask God to quiet your jealous and suspicious nature. Stop trying to second-guess every decision your wife or girlfriend has to make on her own. Give them space to make the decisions they need to. Caring is not the same as controlling. Keep on caring, but stop the controlling. Ask God to help you figure out when to let go of relationships that may never be healed.

5. *Ask God to help you be a better man. And then show it.* You may be asking God to help you change—and change may already be happening—but your family has no way of knowing it's for real. Demonstrate consistent change and concern for them. Keep showing a steady interest in their lives. If you have children and you love them, ask God to help you keep up a steady communication with them. Be disciplined in the way you show your family your love. Remember, it's not all about you!

6. *Finally, ask God to lead you to a new "spiritual family."* God will provide you with brothers you never knew you had, with some spiritual fathers that you only dreamed about. They're available around you, if you have

the courage to seek them out and the humility to learn from them. In fact, they're praying right now for God to lead guys like you into their life. They're not a replacement for your natural family—and they don't want to be. They're a bonus, an extra gift from God.

Think About It. Talk About It.

1. What words would you use to describe your relationship with your family before you were locked up? How about after you were locked up? Has it gotten better or worse?

a) strong and healthy

b) cold and distant

c) chaotic

d) lots of fighting

e) I burned my bridges

f) what relationship?   g) other

2. What effect has your incarceration had on your family? How would you guess that they're feeling right now?

a) ashamed

b) depressed and numb

c) fearful for what happens next

d) relieved that you're off the street and

e) angry over what happened   still alive

f) all of the above

3. As you look at the list of practical suggestions for how you might love your family right now, which ones do you think you might need to start working on?

4. Are you open to having new spiritual brothers and fathers while you're in prison? If not, why not? If so, ask God to lead you to them.

From Where I Sit: What It's Like for Me When You're Locked Up; Family Members of Inmates

From a Father

In a way, I could see it coming. I held eternal hope that this would pass you by. I know you tried hard to make it work, but as the strikes started adding up against you it became more difficult to just live in the regular world. Tragically, your options for a normal life became fewer and fewer.

My biggest fear isn't that you get hurt; I know you can handle those types of situations. I fear that you will forget how much I care about you. I fear that you will think I have forgotten about you. I fear that I will not hear you laugh anymore.

I really look forward to you letters and especially your phone calls. I can hear in your voice when you have to be cold and hard-nosed—not to me but to the others around you to survive.

I try to remember you as the person I know. I catch myself thinking after a week or so has passed what your week has been like. The things I take for granted are luxuries to you. I feel guilty for not wanting to know all you are going through.

I am grateful for your faith in God. I am grateful that this has made me depend on God more and more. I have learned how little we are actually in control and thank God that he is. I am grateful that you will still be a relatively young man when you get out. I completely trust that God will take care of you for the rest of your life.

I pray that you pray. I pray that God will put other Christians in your path and that you can be there for others. I pray that you truly understand that you have been forgiven and that you nail your guilt to the cross. I pray that you will be able to occupy the time spent lying awake in the dark with memories that make your heart glad. I pray that as a parent I was able to make enough happy memories for you to carry you through.

Don't ever forget that you are my son; I will always love you.

From a Mother

While I am heart-broken that you are in prison, I am grateful that I know where you are, and that you are (hopefully) safe and can get some help. I grieve for your lost time and opportunities, while hoping that this time will set you on a positive path with a future. I want to be supportive, but I feel helpless. I am also still angry, and at the same time very sad.

Each time you have had encounters with the legal system, it has been the result of doing things we counseled you over and over against. So there is anger and disappointment on our side, as well as shame. I'm sure there are many people who, fortunately, have not had these experiences and feel the parents are the ones who have failed their child by not providing enough proper teaching and discipline. It certainly haunts me. What if I had been a different personality, what if I worked less, what if we had been more strict, or more lenient, or moved to a different place, or . . .

The list is endless. But in the end I can change nothing, and must let go of the what ifs and stop caring what anyone who has not been through this thinks. I love you, and always want good things for you. I just don't know how to help you accomplish that anymore. I pray for all of you boys, and so do many other people. I will just have to wait for God and the Holy Spirit to work.

I want you to feel you have my support, but I don't want you to feel like I can do anything to change your situation. You have not confided in us truthfully, and I cannot think of one time you asked us to help. We have tried to connect you with resources, but so far you have consumed them without seeming to get on to a successful track. Who knows where you would have been without them, however. I want you to feel that I will help you, but there is an element of self-preservation on my part, too. Aside from the financial carnage you can cause, there is the heartbreak each time you stumble. So while I want to hold out my arms to you, I cannot help you if I am also drowning.

You are physically far from home. Other than providing outrageously priced snacks, visits use vacation days, gasoline and energy without changing anything. I want to be supportive, but I do not want to lessen the consequences of your choices. Quality time with your family has been available to you for years, but you have rarely taken advantage of that. Why? Is it fear of our judgment? Can't stand the thought of another lecture?

So I will endeavor to write more regularly. I will fill the pages with family news. I want you to know what everyone is doing, and what you could be doing, or will be invited to do again when you are available. I will not put my life on hold. That would be a waste of the time and gifts God has given. I will depend on other people to counsel you and I will pray for your maturity and your safety. I will try to send pictures regularly. I want you to be able to see us, and to share photos with your peers. I also want you to have a vision of yourself playing with your kids, traveling with us, working, participating in life. But this vision cannot be passive. You have to pursue your own vision.

All I ever want for any of my children is happiness, peace, purpose and a chance to share love. Use all your gifts to chase a positive goal, not just to survive day to day. See something through all the way to the finish. Don't give up on yourself, or us, or God. We're still here. Waiting.

Love,

Mom

From a Father

I am sad that you are in such a useless space. Life is so short with so much to see, experience and try to figure out, and there you are, waiting, doing your time until you are again a free man.

A father wants his son to shoulder his own weight, to take pride in his own worth and find value in others. I want you to look at the world and see the value God places on you and the guy standing next to you. I want you see the value of working toward your goals knowing you may not achieve them, but it's the lives that you touch and touch you while you try that are ultimately important. This can only be done with the help of the Lord. Ask for his help.

I am angry because I tried to instill these things in you, but you have chosen to take a selfish path hurting not only yourself but all the people around you.

A father wants his son to know love, the love of God, the love of a mate, the love of children and the joy that comes from nurturing that love. It takes great labor, a labor of love. I want you to know love, to seek it out, to strive mightily to maintain it. This can only be done with God's help. Ask for his help.

I am afraid because I can do virtually nothing to keep you safe or help you to grow while you are there or when you get out.

A father loves his child but comes to know he is not God; he cannot keep his child safe from harm, the harm of others or himself. I know you are hurting. I know you were hurting and that's why you are there now. I cannot stop your hurt. God loves you more, and more perfectly, than I. He can stop the hurt. Ask for his help.

I am hopeful because I know you. I know that wonderful person that God means you to be. I have seen him when the hurt was less. I am hoping that person is the man you become. I also know through God all things are possible. I pray every day God will help you become that person. Son, ask God to help.

Love,

Dad

Being a Man, Being a Father

At some level, everybody in here struggles to answer the question about manhood. It's going on all the time when we interact with each other. We're competing and testing ourselves and each other. On one level we're looking for *strength*. Who's strong? Who isn't? No one wants to be seen as soft.

But it's not only physical strength we're testing in each other. We're also sizing each other up to see *strength of character*, to see who's trustworthy. We wonder, "Can I trust this guy with my stuff?" Our starting point is a skeptical one. We think, "I'm not gonna listen to what you're saying. I'm gonna watch your footsteps and see what you do over time. Then, and only then, am I gonna listen."

What makes you a man? Chances are, if you ask ten guys this question you'll get ten different answers. Popular cultural wisdom, for example, celebrates and promotes the myth of the "successful man." Whether you measure success by wealth or possessions or career or status, it's all about "more." In this way of thinking, being a man means keeping score, beating the opposition, and racking up victory after victory. Being a man means being "a winner." This is the myth that the true meaning and measure of a man is how well he charts on "lifestyles of the rich and famous."

What popular cultural wisdom doesn't tell us is that this endless and single-minded pursuit of success just leaves most guys empty. The fruits of their success lose their flavor, or they never brought the level of satisfaction that they expected. That's why so many guys who are considered successes shift the focus of their lives *away from* success and towards something more significant. They want their lives to matter, to make a difference.

Many of us, of course, never bought into the myth of the "successful man." We never thought we had much of a chance of that, or we thought the game was rigged. Instead, we bought into an alternate myth about ourselves, the one that the streets teach us. We grew up thinking that men are supposed to be strong, to demand respect, and to have their way with women. We call this a myth because all you have to do is look around: How well is that working for you and all the guys around you?

You know the drill. You listen to the conversation on the deck or in the yard, talking about how tough we were, how we didn't take crap from anyone, how we left a string of children behind us. We do this in order to display our strength, our honor, and our sexual ability—signs of being a real man. But the truth is, when you strip away the b.s., all it proves is that most of us never grew up at all. The reality is, we have behaved like confused, hurt, aimless, foolish, impatient, undisciplined, addicted, lonely, unhappy, and irresponsible children. Lots of us have gotten older, but not really wiser. We still haven't matured. And that's because the streets will never produce a real man. Think about it: You wouldn't plant a young tree in a pile of rocks and glass and expect it to grow up into a healthy tree. You'd just end up with something stunted and twisted. Why in the world would we plant a boy on a street corner and expect him to grow up into a healthy man? The streets tell us to be strong, respected, sexual men. But what they create are guys who are brutal, ego-centric and irresponsible. *That's being a man?*

What we men need is a revolution in the definition of manhood. What we need is a serious alternative to the pop-culture myth of the successful man or the street myth of the strong man. The biblical vision of being a man doesn't get caught up in either myth. Jesus didn't call men to follow him so that we could make a pile of money or be the toughest guy on the block. Jesus didn't call men to follow him so that they could mess up anybody who disrespected them. Jesus knew that men who follow him already have their own inner sense of self-respect that comes from knowing that God loves them and that God wants to do something important through them. Jesus calls men to a different way to be a man—to live a fruitful life. Jesus was talking about the qualities of our character. St. Paul puts it this way, "The fruit of the Spirit is love, joy, peace, patience, kindness, generosity, faithfulness, gentleness, and self-control" (Galatians 5:22-23).

In a way, what each one of us needs to do is to pick his fruit. The fruits of success inevitably grow tasteless and don't satisfy. The fruits of the streets grow bitter and go rotten. But the fruits of the Spirit just keep growing sweeter and feed others. You're a man: this is a decision you need to make for your own life. Do you want to be an empty suit, a street hustler, or God's man? Choose your fruit, and what kind of man you want to be, and plant yourself there.

The father-problem. Let's be honest and just deal with this issue head-on. We have a serious "father problem" on our hands. It probably afflicts 99% of the guys who are locked up, and lots of guys who aren't. Sometimes the problem is "the father I never knew." Lots of us never had any meaningful relationship with our biological fathers. They were missing in action. For the rest of us, our problem was "the dysfunctional father I did know"— who was unreliable, untrustworthy, disengaged, drunk, or violent.

Either way—whether our fathers were absent or dysfunctional—we were wounded as boys. This isn't just some psycho-babble. This is the honest-to-God truth. As boys, we didn't get the fatherly love and support we needed. We didn't get the practical wisdom we needed. We didn't have a father around to model healthy, godly living for us. Over the years, lots of us responded to that wound by going into denial mode: "He didn't care about me. I don't care about him."

But we did care, of course. We were hurt, ashamed, or filled with rage. But since we were taught to be "strong," we covered up our feelings. We were told that we had to be "the man of the house," but nobody ever showed us what that was supposed to look like. Truth was, we were simply too young too take on such a huge responsibility. We still needed fathering ourselves. And so, instinctively, some of us found ourselves drawn to the gang to find acceptance and support, to try to grab some of what we were missing from our real fathers.

Let's be clear on this: we are not saying that our fathers are to blame for the situation we find ourselves in. That would be a lie and a cop-out. But at the same time, we do need to face up to the ugly truth that, for many of us, those childhood wounds inflicted by our absent or dysfunctional fathers are real and deep and have never properly healed. We're not going to get better until we wise up and realize this fundamental fact. Unless we men see the truth of what we're doing to each other and deal with it (including finding a way to forgive it), we're just going to keep on repeating the same ugly cycle with our own kids.

That brings us to the question of how well we're doing as fathers. One guy recently told us, "Anybody can be a dad, but only one man can be a kid's biological father." He was feeling cut off from one of his daughters but still proudly holding on to the fact that he was her biological father. We understand his point, but we think that's exactly backward thinking! Let's face it: most any guy can get a woman pregnant. It's not all that difficult. But we think it takes a real man to be that child's dad—to be that providing, nurturing influence day in and day out.

You may be thinking, "Yes! That's exactly what I want to do. I want to begin to break the cycle and begin to be a better dad now!" You may long to be like the father in the book of Proverbs who says things like, "My child, if you accept my words ..." or "My child, do not forget my teaching ..." or "My child, be attentive to my wisdom ..." (check out the first eight chapters of the book of Proverbs, right in the middle of the Bible). But here's the thing: the voice of the wise father in the book of Proverbs also said, "When I was a son with my father, tender, and my mother's favorite, he taught me and said to me, 'Let your heart hold fast to my words; keep my commandments, and live." The problem is, few of us had that same experience. We didn't grow up with a wise father. We certainly weren't treated tenderly by him. We weren't taught his wisdom or how to live by his commandments. For us, the chain of wisdom was a *broken* one.

So, instead of having wise fathers who handed on their wisdom, we had absent or dysfunctional fathers. And now we have to face up to the fact that we ourselves are the current generation of absent and dysfunctional fathers.

So what can we do to change things? For those of us who have children, what can we do about changing ourselves, about being more present, more functional, and more wise fathers?

First of all, while we're incarcerated, there's only so much we can do about being physically absent. No one is going to open the prison gates so that we can go and play with our kids or help them with their homework. But what we can begin to do is to send signals to our kids that we care and *that we want to be present.* We can begin to write, consistently. We can ask a lot of personal questions and then really pay attention when they answer. We can begin to pray for them, daily. We realize that this is still inadequate, and that our kids really need our physical presence, but it's a healthy start. We can start behaving now in the way we're going to be when we can be physically present again.

As for becoming more functional and wise as fathers, there's a lot we can do about that right now too. The goal is to become fathers who pass on our love and our wisdom to our kids. But the problem is, we can't give what we don't have. If we're honest, we have to admit that most of us don't have a lot of excess love and wisdom inside. If the best gift we can ever give our kids is a wise and loving father, then the best way to do that is for us to begin to be in touch with our wise and loving heavenly Father. Our earthly fathers may have left us. But our heavenly Father hasn't. Our earthly fathers may have been absent. But our heavenly Father is always there for us. Our earthly fathers may have wasted their chance at fatherhood. But our heavenly Father is a God of second chances, and is giving us a chance to learn from him what it is to be wise and loving. There's still time to become the father your children need.

God ain't gonna let you get out till you're ready. Don't go back where you came from if you don't have to; you're someone valuable and you still have a chance for a different life; stick with your kids—deny yourself and care for them; find your higher power; forgive!
—Anonymous

I didn't get serious about my faith till I met a kid who needed to hear me say I loved Jesus. That's when he started trusting God. We've got to stop at some time saying "me, me, me."
—Rodney

If you get fathering right it'll change your kids and change you. God gave me my father when he sent me to prison.
—Anonymous

From Where I Sit: Tom Beatty, Director of New Life Corrections Ministry

Listen to some words of wisdom from Tom Beatty, a former inmate and now a prison chaplain, on being a man and a father.

We inmates (and former inmates) are handicapping our kids!

There are 2.2 million children under 18 now who have at least one incarcerated parent. Children of inmates are about 7 times more likely to be incarcerated than their peers. And kids from "fatherless homes" are

- 67 times more likely to be arrested by age 12

- 32 times more likely to run away

- 20 times more likely to have behavioral disorders

- 14 times more likely to commit rape

- 10 times more likely to abuse alcohol/drugs

- 5 times more likely to commit suicide

I learned how to be a father in the home in which I was raised. I do **not** blame my dad; it's just that the way I was raised didn't work out so well—I became an inmate, an addict, a drunk. But since I was now a Christian, I wanted to raise my kids differently.

God was good to me. He provided a church where the men of the church kind of "adopted" me. They didn't make it appear like they did—they probably didn't even know that they did—but as a group of men, they displayed for me how to be a Christian man, husband and dad. I'm sure I didn't pick up all they wanted me to learn, but without them I'd have been on my own. They were great!

Not all inmates are going to get out soon and have the opportunities I had. But the changes have to start while we're "in" and continue when we're "out." So, here are some things to think on:

There's only one perfect Father: God! The Bible is full of references to God as our Father, and ultimately, we learn how to be a father from God. We learn to relate to our kids the way our Father God relates to us as his kids. We must allow our relationship with God to be the model for our relationships with our kids.

The best thing we can give our kids is a good example! If we're going to be good examples to our kids, we have to have good examples for our own selves. This means being choosy about who and where we're going to allow ourselves to be around! Start the habit of church attendance while you're still in. And try to not settle for just "church attendance." Aim for church involvement!

Allow your kids to "catch" you! Did you ever notice how kids imitate their parents? The values we want our kids to have will be more "caught" than "taught." One **huge** thing our kids need to catch from us is a feeling of security. They need to have faith in us. They need to be able to depend upon us. This goes back to allowing our relationship with God to be the model for our relationships with our kids. Are you secure in your faith relationship with Jesus Christ? Let me ask it in a different way: Is your faith "well-placed"? I observe too many people with "mis-placed" faith.

My sheep listen to My voice; I know them, and they follow Me. I give them eternal life, and they shall never perish; no one can snatch them out of My hand. My Father, who has given them to Me, is greater than all; no one can snatch them out of My Father's hand. I and the Father are one. [John 10:27-30]

Jesus gives his sheep eternal life. Who are his sheep? All who have received him, repented of their sins, and trusted in him as Lord and Savior. Think on this: We are not his sheep because we follow him. **We follow him because we are his sheep.**

Jesus says no one can snatch his sheep out of his hand. We don't have security because we hold onto him. We have security because he holds onto us! If my faith is in **me** holding onto Jesus, it's mis-placed. There's no security in mis-placed faith. But if my faith is in Jesus holding onto me, it's well-placed faith!

Bless your kids with a feeling of security! Don't expect them to be secure because they hold tightly to you. No, allow your kids to find security in you holding tightly to them!

Think About It. Talk About It.

1. When you were a boy, which men did you look up to? Were they "successful," "strong," or "spiritual" men?

2. What would you say are the essential qualities of being a real man?

3. What was your relationship with your biological father like? Was he present, or was he missing in action? Was he stable, or was he messed up? Did you ever have a step-father or a foster father? If so, what were they like?

4. Looking back, what effect has your own "father problem" had on your life?

5. Are you a father yourself? If so, how well are you doing at that role? What could you do better or differently while you're incarcerated? How could you help your kids feel more secure and know that you truly love them?

6

KEEPING IT GOING:
Moving Beyond Survival Mode

Sometimes we have a way of getting in the way of ourselves and of God's work in us.
—Anthony

I find myself taunted and tested, and that can be difficult at times.
—Jacques

My biggest challenge has been putting all of my problems in the Lord's hand. I still hold some things back.
—Doaikah

Prison is hard. If someone tells you it's not, they are not telling the truth—to you or to themselves. Having God in your life is a good thing, but it doesn't make prison easy. If you think it will, you should think again, like Dan did:

I thought that because I'd made a decision to live a spiritual life, all or most of my pain would go away. That didn't happen. I've learned to keep going—one day at a time, doing my best.

Someone once said, "God does not want to make life easy. God wants to make us great." That includes prison, and after prison, when you get out. Not "great" in the way that famous people are great; more like the people you grew up thanking God for, people you know are good.

Prison is hard. But God is on your side. God wants to help you in prison to become great. God does that by giving you things—things like prayer, a Bible, time to think—and by giving you people—people who believe God is on their side and who want God to make them, and you, great.

Biggest Challenges and Frustrations

It's hard—maybe impossible—to prepare for a place like prison. It's a very different place from home, school, work or anywhere else. But by now, you already understand that. Somehow you've managed to cope with the everyday foolishness, the physical discomfort, the food, the endless rules and regulations, and so on. But beyond those everyday challenges and frustrations, there are some others that eat away at you spiritually. The inmates we talked to faced the challenges you'll be facing.

Time to yourself. "It hurts to look in the mirror and see the person who destroyed my future." That's what Doiakah found most challenging. Your time inside means time with yourself. Maybe at times you'll feel trapped with yourself. You'll think about decisions you made, people you hurt, people who hurt you. You'll wonder what's happening with your family and friends on the outside, and you'll wish they came by or wrote more often. Meanwhile, you have yourself to keep you company, and you may get tired of yourself.

That's normal. We were made for friendship, for connection. But we were also made to depend on God. God gives us time alone so that we can remember him and relate to him directly, without having to put up a front.

Alone with God we can be ourselves, not dressed up in the rep we've crafted for ourselves.

Alone with God we can admit when we're lonely, when we're scared, when we're tired, when we're angry. We can admit our weakness, knowing that God is strong and God is for us.

In fact, the prophet Isaiah promises that God "gives strength to the weary and increases the power of the weak" (Isaiah 40:29). Or, as Volney learned from his time alone with God, "God can deliver me from anything."

Loneliness. Time alone with God is great, but it doesn't change the fact that we were made to be friends. "It's not good . . . to be alone," the Bible says. But prison is a tough place to find, make and keep friends. James, in fact, called prison "as lonely a place as a man could be."

Prison doesn't have to be lonely. But you'll have to work at it. You're surrounded by thousands of people, each with a story, from the officers to the inmates. A good friend in prison can make all the difference: people who make good friends will have a generally good experience; people who make bad friends will have a generally bad experience.

What's a "good friend," though? It's not just someone who has your back. Lots of people will recruit you to be their "friends"; they'll do favors for you and expect favors in return. The gangs, for instance. Gangs in prison are little more than friends who are indebted to each other. Gang friends will have your back, but their protection comes at a cost. That's bad friendship. Bad friends lack patience and kindness. They envy and brag. They're arrogant and self-serving; they set you up when it serves them. Bad friends look for reasons to break trust, and they don't forget—or let you forget—when you slip up with them. Bad friends enjoy getting themselves—and you—into trouble, and they'll cover their tracks even if you wind up having to pay for their bad behavior. You'll know when a friendship is breaking bad when you don't feel secure, don't feel hopeful, don't feel encouraged by how your "friend" is relating to you.

Maybe that's why the inmates we interviewed all said that one of the most important things to their spiritual survival was friendship with older inmates who looked after them. Older inmates may have less to prove. They may have learned from enough mistakes to know better. They may just be tired of false friends and looking for the real deal. In any case, almost every inmate we talked to said they were *blessed* by older men who treated them well and showed them the ropes without asking for anything in return. If you can find a friend like that, it'll make keeping your head up a lot easier. You may even learn something. But at the very least, you'll have a friend, which as the Bible says, is a good thing.

Being a "work in progress." Ask anyone, inside or outside prison, and if they're honest, they'll admit that some of their greatest frustrations and challenges come from dealing with *themselves*. We start each morning with great hopes and expectations, but by the end of the day we find that we've let ourselves (and God) down once again.

Sometimes it's a case of willpower. Sometimes it's a case of staying power. Sometimes it's a case of dealing with those old demons in our lives that aren't leaving without another big fight—all those thoughts and fears that come rushing at us when the lights go out at night. It's frustrating to realize that we're still dealing with lots of the same of things that we were years before.

The Lord tells us that we're "under construction," and that we're a work in progress. In our heads we know that's true—and it helps. But in our hearts, it's frustrating. Sometimes we want to say, "Hurry up, Lord! Finish this construction project in me. And quick!"

The frustration and challenge isn't only for ourselves. We may really be trying our best, but from a distance what others see in us is hypocrisy. That's the real frustration. Melvin writes,

> It's easier for Christians to hide outside; it's much harder to be a Christian inside, because you're on display in close quarters. When you're a follower of Christ in prison, all eyes are on you. So, if you're not going to open yourself to a person, then don't give them the Christian message. God is the perfect example of the man you're supposed to be, because you were made in his image. You're always on mission.

Melvin's right. We're on display, we're talking the talk, we're on a mission—but we still have to deal with our lingering imperfections. We asked some of the guys what they're still frustrated by in themselves. See if you can relate to what they're saying:

What I still find hard is just dealing with life on life's terms—and facing my own impatience and my selfish self. Sometimes we have a way of getting in the way of ourselves and of God's work in us.
—Anthony

I still struggle with just "being still," and waiting patiently for things to happen.
—Volney

My biggest challenge still comes from wanting to hold on to the outward respect that I used to get from officers and inmates back when I had a position in the gang. I find myself taunted and tested, and that can be difficult at times.
—Jacques

My biggest challenges are me not witnessing as I should, still struggling with lust for women, feeling anxious and doubting, and living obediently according to God's Word. A lot of my disappointments are in myself because I'm not giving 100 percent to God and I know that I should be giving him my all.
—Anonymous

One of my biggest challenges has been to be a genuine, sincere person. I've had a hard time trusting others too much. I've learned that if I share something or some time with someone, then I've often had to pull back some.
—Robert

Sometimes when I pray, I think God will carry out my will—right there and then. I forget so easily that prayer is getting up to fall in line to do God's will, not some magic formula to get him to do our will.
—Jose

One of the things that these guys turn to as they deal with these frustrations is . . . each other. God has wired us for relationship, for true community. God invites us (in fact, he commands us) to be there for one another—to build each other up, encourage each other, hold each other accountable, comfort each other, teach and coach each other, and tell each other the truth both when it's sweet and when it stings. In a word, God calls us to love each other—to be part of a band of brothers.

If you've ever experienced it, there's nothing better than to be surrounded by a band of brothers who will pick you up when you're down, who will gently bring you down when you get too full of yourself, who will have your back when you're under attack, and who will protect your confidences. The guys who do well spiritually in prison find trustworthy friends who will be part of their band of brothers.

Still, sometimes even our band of brothers lets us down. And that can be really frustrating, challenging, even devastating.

I've been disappointed by certain brothers who claim to be true Christians and followers of Christ, yet they prey on other Christians for money, commissary, or information to use against that brother or against others.
—Kevin

A recurring disappointment is seeing others fall from God's holy calling to them or simply taking it lightly.
—Jose

It's disappointing that more brothers don't want to take the righteous path seriously.
—Kentes

Dealing with unreliable Christians is like being on a basketball team and finding out that half the guys on your team won't bother to suit up. Or they'll suit up, but once they get on the floor they won't hustle, focus, or play defense. They treat it like it's no big deal. It can drive you crazy, because you really thought you were a unit. You thought you were in it together. The truth is, we can get a lot more frustrated and let-down by our own teammates than by the other team!

But other than demanding perfection and refusing to have anything to do with each other, what can do we do about that?

There's a passage in the Bible that talks about how judgment begins with the family of God (1 Peter 4:17). Jesus calls all of his followers to examine themselves first, and only afterward look at the faults of their brothers. Once we've done that (and that's something we need to do every day), we can begin to make that family judgment call. (Check out Jesus teaching about the "speck" and the "log" in Luke 6:41-42.)

There are at least three varieties of unreliable Christians in jail.

The first group are the *"fronters,"* the false, deceptive, and counterfeit Christians. God knows what these brothers are really up to, but whatever it is, it's not following Jesus in any real way. The biblical model for dealing with these men is to lovingly but firmly confront them—to make it clear that they need to stop the phoniness.

The second (and far larger) group of unreliable Christians are the *weak and inconsistent* ones. These are the brothers who get it one day and then seem to forget it the next. They're like a great car with an iffy battery. One day they'll start right up, and the next day they're completely dead. These brothers need a recharge, need to get a jump-start.

Most of us are in this category sometimes, so the best approach to this group is a balance of both encouragement (a boost to their spiritual energy) and accountability (a firm reminder that what we do matters).

The final group of unreliable Christians are the *immature and beginner* Christians. These guys are like kids who are learning to ride a bike. You just have to expect that they're going to be falling and crashing and making a fool of themselves. Becoming a follower of Jesus is a process of trial and error. Nobody gets it perfectly at first. And if you doubt that, then just read the Gospel stories and see how poorly Jesus' first immature and beginner disciples did.

The best approach for dealing with beginners is to give them room to explore, to experiment, to try things out for themselves. They don't need somebody standing off to the side laughing at them or angrily pointing the finger. But they sure could use some cheerleading, some help getting back up again when they fall, and some encouragement that they'll get the hang of it one day.

Of course, all of this raises the question: How do we know which person falls into what category? How can we tell if someone else is immature, inconsistent, or false?

That's a great question. And it doesn't have an easy answer. In fact, Jesus' first followers wondered about the same thing. And he told them a story (what is often called a parable) that basically said, "Tread very carefully here. Give it time. You don't want to stumble in with your judging and do more harm than good. God will sort the whole thing out when it's time." (See how Jesus put it in Matthew 13:24-30.)

In A.A. we say not to so much listen to what people say but "watch their feet" — see what they do.
—Dan

"Never quite enough." It can be truly frustrating to always be having to "make do." Jesus invites us to follow him and live an "abundant" life, but there never seems to be quite enough abundance of the good things in prison. It's like the frustration of not having enough food or drink to ever fill you up properly. You walk away from a meal having been fed but not truly satisfied. You've had a drink, but you still feel thirsty.

What's true of food and drink also seems to hold for lots of guys when it comes to relationships and outside support. Letters and visits from loved ones sometimes only make us miss them more. We take part in a program in the prison, but it seems to be over in no time. We make some deep spiritual friends, but the institution periodically yanks them away for no apparent reason.

Here's what our guys mentioned ...

I'm disappointed that I'm not able to be more hands-on with my family members. It's one thing for them to hear me talk the talk, but I believe that if they could see me walk the walk it would make a big difference in their lives.
            —Duncan

I don't have a church or consistent outside support group, so I'm forced to live in a state of poverty. I feel helpless and frustrated that no one seems to be concerned or able to help me with my personal needs.
            —JT

It's disappointing to think that society in general has pretty much given up those of us in prison. Also, the lack of programs for rehabilitation instead of warehousing.
            —James

It's incredibly difficult when you're in the gallery with fellow brothers in Christ for years and the placement office ends up moving you for some reason. Now you have to start all over again to try and build relationships with new people.
—Wilfredo

I'm frustrated by my family not being here for me to tell me they love me.
—Timothy

Think About It. Talk About It.

1. How big a challenge is it for you to be alone with your thoughts? Does it feel good to stop and really think for a change, or does it drive you crazy?

2. How do you deal with your loneliness?

a) I distract myself
b) I try to stay busy
c) I seek out other people, even if I know they're bad for me
d) I take those feelings to God in prayer
e) other

3. Do you find it helpful to think of three varieties of unreliable Christians (false, weak, and immature)? Does that help to explain some of the guys you've met? How about you? Do you get frustrated with your own unreliability?

4. How do you usually handle the frustration of "never quite enough"? What, if anything, could you begin to do differently to ease those frustrations?

Listening to this long list of challenges and frustrations might lead you to think that nothing truly good can ever happen in prison, and that the only good day is the day the gate swings open and you walk out. But that's just not true. Thank God that there are all kinds of positive things going on inside. Lives are truly being changed. Deep transformation is going on. There are blessings and surprises and joyful moments to praise God for. Let's look at some of them.

Biggest Surprises and Joys

So much of prison life revolves around long periods of "routine," punctuated by crazy, out-of-control incidents, followed by mind-numbing lockdowns, followed by—you guessed it, another long period of "routine." But in the middle of that big, predictable, overall cycle, God can have lots of surprises and joys in store for us, if we know where to look. At the beginning of this *Spiritual Survival Guide* we talked about the "lights-on" guys you come across in prison. They have learned where to find surprising and joyful things and moments. Here are the top four things they told us about.

We can actually change. It's a funny thing: We can yearn and hope and pray for something for so long that we're actually surprised when we finally get it. Often, we just catch glimpses of how we're changing inside. Just as our "bad side" can remain hidden from us, so can our new, "God-shaped" side. Most of the time we're so focused on what hasn't happened yet that we tend to overlook what has *already* happened.

Real change takes time. We overestimate what we can change in a year, but we also underestimate what God can do in us over five years. Listen to some very surprised changed men—men who found new beginnings, contentment, humility, sanity, peace, joy, self-love, and a bright future.

I've had many surprises over the years. The first one is when I backed away from the gang in here. There were other members who wanted or did take that same leap of faith—it started a big thing in here.
—Jacques

I'm surprised that I can feel content, that I can humble myself, and that I can still have a sound mind.
—JT

After so much hardship and hurt, my biggest surprise is that I was able to find true peace. Not to say that I don't have bad days—I do—but I now have the calm of the Holy Spirit.
—Doaikah

My biggest surprise and joy has been learning who I really am. God has revealed to me my true identity: I've had to get used to this new man who I'd never met before. He is wonderful!
—Rodney

I'm surprised that I am not the same person that I used to be eight years ago; that Christ loves me; that I can now talk to people about God; that I will be home soon to teach this amazing Word of God to my wife and kids.
—Timothy

Being in a stressful place like this—enough to drive a sane man berserk—the biggest surprise is that I can actually have joy in my life! God is good!
—Kentes

True spiritual friends. Just as a lot of us never truly thought we'd see deep change in our souls a few years ago, we also never thought we'd find other men who truly knew how to be a positive, healthy, loyal,

God-fearing friend. You may have walked into prison filled with sus-
picion, with your self-protective defenses jacked up a mile high, determined never to show weakness, trusting nothing and no one. Maybe
you looked into the faces of the men around you and thought, *Keep
your distance.* Maybe you felt terribly alone.

But God had other plans in store. He can lead us out of our isolation to
men who know what it is to be a friend, who want nothing for us but
the best. God can show us men we can trust with our thoughts and feelings; men to share both awful and wonderful days; men who tell it like
it is and whom we can listen to, because we know they care about and
respect us deep down.

And when the time is right, God will surprise us by turning us into
trustworthy spiritual men who then lead new men to Jesus and watch
Jesus do what only Jesus can do in a man.

I have met some genuine Christian brothers in here. It's a joy to be
able to share some of my life experiences with other Christians.
—Robert

It gave me joy (and still does) to see some of these young guys in
here whom I knew when they were gang members who've given
their life to the Lord and watched them grow in their spiritual
knowledge and their love for God.
—Jacques

It's a joy that God changes things and a surprise that God uses
other people to help me.
—Volney

Just seeing another man turn his life over to (or back to) God is probably the most gratifying thing.
  —James

It's a surprise that I have actually found true Christians here who have shared their trials and turmoil along with mine.
  —Nathaniel

New depths and heights of understanding. A huge surprise for most guys is how many levels of understanding there are in the life of faith. God's truth is like a diamond—every little turn makes a new facet shine, sending off new rays of light. It's like going up the Sears Tower—every new floor allows you to see things you couldn't have seen before. You get a whole new perspective. You can make new connections. You can look down at your life, your past, your neighborhood, the streets, all of it—and see it from God's perspective. And through it all, you can glimpse God's mighty, unshakable love that loves you no matter what.

There's no bottom to God's truth—it goes far and wide and deep—but it also makes its home in our soul. It has filled that blank or void in my soul that no drug ever could. It's exciting to feel the joy of new believers around me.
  —Jose

It's just amazing to see God at work. He has always come through for me right on time, and he's there for me even when I'm living in my filth at times. He forgives me and is patient with me. He assures me of things. He blesses me. The list goes on and on! It just surprises me and brings me joy that God doesn't give up on me and that he's always faithful even though I don't deserve it.
  —Anonymous

The biggest joy and surprise is that Jesus loves me in spite of myself.
  —Anthony

Think About It. Talk About It.

1. Lots of inmates report that the most surprising thing that happened to them in prison is that they actually changed as men. Would you be surprised if that happened to you, or has God already started that change in you?

2. Do you currently have any spiritual friends inside prison? Outside prison? Would you be surprised by (and would you welcome) more spiritual friends if God led them your way in the next six months?

Prayer Life: Top Ten Things We've Learned

Prayer is the life-blood of our relationship with God. You simply can't overestimate the importance of it for spiritual survival—inside or outside these walls. In fact, some of us found ourselves beginning to pray like crazy only when we got to county lock-up—bargaining with God, hoping to avoid prison time. Others of us never bothered with all that. We thought we were tough and smart, and that prayer was for the weak and foolish. Some of us were in-between the two groups. We weren't against prayer, but we never really understood what it was all about, either.

So what is prayer, anyway? Maybe at its most basic prayer is talking and listening to God. Not *about* God. *To* God. Person to person. Like he was your best and only true friend. Like he was right in the cell with you. Like the creator of the universe had nothing more important to do than to spend personal time with you—to listen to you and communicate with you. Prayer is all about you having a relationship with God and God having a relationship with you.

If you're having problems relating to a God you can't see face to face, then think about whatever it is you'd like to talk about and imagine saying it to Jesus (who is, after all, the human face of God). And then don't just imagine saying it—go ahead and actually say it. Say it out loud if that helps. Say it silently in your mind if that's easier. For most of us, praying can feel weird at first, especially if we didn't pray as children. It can seem as if we're talking into the empty air. Sometimes we can feel foolish. But the overwhelming majority of us have found something beyond the foolishness. We find ourselves feeling strangely free. We feel lifelong burdens lifting. We feel hope begin to stir. We feel insight and direction begin to come our way. We feel in touch with something and someone bigger and more mysterious than ourselves.

We're well aware that this brief description of prayer just raises more questions. That's because, although prayer itself can be the most natural and simple thing, a lifetime of prayer isn't. It's complicated, because *we're* complicated creatures. To help you think about prayer, and then to help you through your own prayer life, we'd like to share some things we've learned, some prayers we treasure, and some prayer patterns that you might want to try out.

Here are the top ten things that we've learned about prayer that you might want to consider.

1. Be yourself. First of all, don't pretend to be someone you're not. Don't fake it. Don't mimic somebody else's spiritual language and style. Don't be intimidated by the "prayer warriors" around you. Don't worry about "doing it right." In fact, we heard someone say one time that "if you're praying, you're already doing it right." We can get ourselves all tied into knots by over-thinking and over-analyzing. That's not what God wants. Just relax and talk the way that you talk and say what's on your heart and mind. You appreciate honest, authentic, straight-up talk, don't you? God does too.

Being honest with God also means telling him what's really on your mind. If you have something specific to tell him, then be specific. Don't hide what you really want. Say, "God, I don't know if it's right or not, but here's what I really want." Don't cover up how you really feel. And if you're frustrated with circumstances or angry with him—then tell him. Again, God really appreciates honesty and can deal with it.

Of course, one of the biggest barriers to "being ourselves" is our pride. Most of us don't like to put our weakness or neediness on display. Our pride makes us cover it up. But it's like having a wound we won't show the doctor: God doesn't heal what we won't uncover. The Bible has great advice on this point. "Humble yourselves therefore under the mighty hand of God, so that he may exalt you in due time. Cast all your anxiety on him, because he cares for you" (1 Peter 5:5-7). How can we ever hope to feel the mighty hand of God who cares for us if we won't show him the real us? Just be yourself.

2. Find your rhythm. Discover what works best for you. For example, some of us can't think straight in the morning, so morning prayers are never going to work well. Some of us are at our best at night. Some of us need twenty minutes just to settle down long enough to begin to pray, so we need to give ourselves plenty of time. When you find yourself running out of things to say to God after five minutes, you may be better off keeping it short.

Try experimenting with different times of day. The morning can be a great time to set up the day and entrust it to God. Lunch break can be a kind of half-way check-in. And the evening can be a good time to review how things have gone. While you're at it, try alternating between praying alone and with someone else (if you can find someone to do this with you). It can be a great encouragement and inspiration to hear and share in the prayers of someone else, especially if you're new to the practice of prayer.

3. Tune in. Often we get so focused on what we want to say to God that we forget to listen. In our rush to be heard, we don't slow down or quiet down enough to pick up what he might be trying to say to us in return. God really wants to listen to us—but he also wants us to be patient enough to listen to what he's saying. The problem is, many of us are not patient people. In fact, there's a famous passage in the Bible that says, "Be still and know that I am God" (Psalm 46:10). The sad truth is, lots of us have gotten ourselves into a world of trouble over the years precisely because we were unwilling to be still, and unwilling to know that God alone was God—and that we weren't.

Prayer can be a time to listen carefully, to tune in to God's wavelength—and to see the world as God sees it. Try visualizing yourself standing alongside God, looking at the world. Imagine how God already feels about things, about how much he already cares, about how much his heart breaks. Open yourself up to a God's-eye view of things. Put things (including your own problems) in this bigger perspective. And then go back and stand in your own situation again. Notice how much smaller your problems look now. Tune in to God's view of things and let it change your own perspective.

One helpful way to be tuned in is to keep track of how often God actually answers prayer. We're usually so busy worrying about "the next thing" that we forget to give thanks for "the last thing"! That's why some people talk about how helpful it's been for them to keep a prayer journal where they jot down what they're praying for so that they can go back later and see how things turned out. More often than not, their prayer journals read

> Something I've done recently is commit to give prayer real time and real thought— to stay away from mindless mumbling.
> —Dan

like an amazing list of answered prayers. Even if you're not the type of person to keep an actual journal, you might want to try keeping a list of blessings. Writing them down can help you notice the small blessings that come your way every day. You might be surprised how long the list can become when you're tuned in to God's goodness.

4. Stretch yourself. It's easy to fall into lazy prayer patterns. We find something that seems to be authentic and works for a while, but over time we can find our prayer life becoming stale or repetitive. When that happens (and it happens to the best of us), trying stretching yourself. You can start expanding your vision of what prayer can look like by exploring the different prayers found in the Bible.

For example, we read that there are around 650 prayers in the Bible. That's a lot of different prayers! So, when you read the Bible, be on the lookout for them. When you come across one, see if you can make it part of your own prayer time. You might be surprised how often you can. Or try reading through the book of Psalms, which is itself a book of prayers. Stretch yourself by making some of those prayers your own.

You might want to try meditating on simple, one-sentence prayers like the fifteen-hundred-year-old Jesus Prayer (*Lord Jesus Christ, Son of God, have mercy on me, a sinner*). Try thinking carefully about a couple of words at a time.

If you normally pray by using memorized prayers, try praying from the heart. If you normally pray off the top of your head, you might find that using a more formal, written-out prayer guide for a month will recharge your prayer life. If you tend to be a chatterbox when you pray, consider just "hanging out" with God sometimes, without words. Just show up and say, "God, I'm just going to spend the next ten minutes here with you." Just like hanging out with a good friend, silence can be okay sometimes.

You might want to shake things up by praying in ever-widening circles and then in ever-narrowing circles. For example, one day you could begin by praying for yourself, then for your celly, then for your tier, then for your cell block, then for your prison, then for your city (your friends and loved ones), and then for the wider world. The next day, you could reverse the process and begin by praying for what's happening in the world and slowly work your way back to yourself. Or try the circles of praying for yourself, your loved ones, and then your enemies. Jesus taught and commanded us to pray for those who persecute us, and there's hardly anything that'll stretch us and grow our faith more than that.

Remember, the point isn't to just bounce around trying anything and everything. The point is to find ways that can keep the lines of communication between you and God fresh, honest, and meaningful.

5. Aim for balance. If prayer is all about our communicating with God, then it's good to check ourselves from time to time to see if we seem to be fixated on just one thing. A healthy relationship with God includes four essential things: giving thanks, asking for help, seeking forgiveness, and praising him for who he is. Sometimes, when things are difficult, we'll go through a phase where all we seem to do is to ask for help. Or maybe we'll be struggling with past guilt and need to keep asking God for forgiveness for a while. That's normal and healthy.

But if that's all we do for an extended period, we can miss out on a fuller relationship with God. Over time it's important to bring balance to how we talk to God. The very act of giving him praise or saying thank you can lift our spirits, help us to see God in a more balanced way, and bring us a tremendous amount of joy and satisfaction. Think about how you normally pray. Is your prayer life lopsided? Are you always asking, but rarely saying thanks? Are you saying thank you, but never saying I'm sorry? Do you tend to say, "God, you're great" but fail to say, "God, please help me?" God is eager to hear all of those things from you, so try to keep balanced.

6. Be persistent. And 7. Respect God's "no."

These two need to be taken together. On the one hand, Jesus tells us to be persistent in prayer. He was always praising people who relentlessly asked for what they needed. He encourages us to ask, and seek, and knock. He didn't tell us to pray once and then let it go.

It's important to remember Jesus' command to be persistent, because we often find ourselves becoming discouraged or weary in prayer. It's hard to keep asking for the same thing over and over. It's emotionally tiring to keep seeking guidance time after time and still come up with no clear plan. That's why the Bible keeps urging us to be "devoted" in prayer and to "pray without ceasing" (1 Thessalonians 5:17). The Christian writer Philip Yancey gives some good advice when he says "keep it short, keep it honest, and keep it going."

At the same time as we need to keep it going, we also need to respect God's answer if it happens to be *No,* or *Not now,* or *I have something different in mind for you.* We all know that not every prayer request is answered by an immediate Yes on God's part. What we don't know is why. The Bible tells us that sometimes God refuses to hear our prayers because they are selfish, inappropriate, or ask him to do something against his nature. The letter of James nails it when it says, "You ask and do not receive because you ask wrongly, in order to spend what you get on your pleasures" (James 4:3).

But sometimes we ask for apparently perfectly appropriate things that God just seems to say no to. This is when prayer gets really tough. St. Paul once talked about how he had some affliction that he called a "thorn in the flesh." He tells how he repeatedly asked God to take away the torment that this affliction was causing him, but that God's answer to him was "My grace is sufficient for you, for power is made perfect in weakness" (2 Corinthians 12:7-10). God was giving him a thorn to prick him so that he wouldn't be too elated. Let's be honest here: This is not a message that most of us want to hear. Who likes thorns? We'd prefer grace and the specific thing we want! But St. Paul found that this affliction was turning out to be a good thing; because of it, the power of Christ was even more effective through him.

The connection between being persistent in prayer and respecting God's No is one word: *Yet.* When Jesus was facing the prospect of betrayal, imprisonment, ridicule, torture and death, he turned to prayer. Again and again and again he prayed that he might avoid taking that path (he referred to it as a cup of suffering). He told his heavenly Father, "Father, if you are willing, remove this cup from me…" He was honest and said what he wanted. He was persistent in praying for what he wanted. But because he was also tuned in to his heavenly Father's will, he completed his prayer by saying, "…*yet,* not my will but yours be done." We'll know that we're making huge progress in our own relationship with God when we can honestly echo Jesus by saying, "God, I really want this—and yet, not my will but yours be done."

8. *Expect dry spells.* Every one of us has some inconsistency when it comes to prayer. We go through seasons. Sometimes, it can seem like spring or summer—that God's right with us in our cell, both surrounding us and welling up from inside us. It can feel as if God's love is gushing up in us. But at other times our prayer life can feel dry as dust. It can seem like a November day—gray, empty, sterile, lifeless. It can sometimes feel like we're praying into nothingness.

Here's the bad news: There's no way around spiritual dry spells. You just have to go through them. Even the greatest saints and spiritual warriors in church history talk about dealing with dry spells. That means that there will almost certainly be times when nothing in your prayer life seems to work. Your prayers will sound hollow and feel empty and pointless. It will feel as if God is deaf or distant. You'll just hit a wall that you can't go around or over or under. You'll be stuck and will start wondering if it'll ever get better. You'll find yourself drawn to prayers like Psalm 13, where it says, "How long, O Lord? Will you forget me forever?"

And now here's the good news: It won't be forever. It does get better. Dry spells end. But it takes patience to work through them. And for most of us, it takes the prayers of other people to get us through. So when you're in a spiritual dry spell, ask other people to pray for you. When your own words seem dry and lifeless, lean on the prayers other people have written. Think about how when a soldier is badly wounded, his buddies don't ignore him or make him rescue himself. They'll risk their own lives to pick him up and carry him to safety. That's how spiritual warfare is, too. When you're feeling spiritually wounded, ask your spiritual buddies to carry you in prayer. If they're willing, ask them to pray out loud for you so that you can feel the power of their words. Don't worry: one day God will let you return the favor for someone else.

9. Be confident and hopeful. The scary thing about prayer is that it quickly exposes two things about us—who we really are, and what we really think about God. The way we talk to God shows whether we think God is a cosmic bellhop, an angry judge, an impersonal, uncaring distant force, or an active, mighty and loving Father.

Some guys pray as if God were a spiritual vending machine: insert two prayers and out pops what you asked for. Some guys swing to the other extreme and treat God like he's a miser who enjoys nothing better than teasing and disappointing his creatures. Other guys have a sense that prayer can actually change things—but only other people's prayer, not their own. They feel like God wouldn't actually listen to them, so why should they even bother. They've lost hope and have really low expectations. They might ask God for something, but in their heart they don't really believe that God would love to give it to them.

> I've done plenty of "Santa Claus" prayers; mostly I've stopped, realizing how immature they are.
> —Dan

But that's just not true. Again and again Jesus taught us that God is eager to help us and show us love. Again and again he taught us not to worry or be anxious. And that's because he knew that our heavenly Father loves us like crazy, and because he can and will use us for something good, true, and significant. We're convinced that it's only when we finally grasp, deep down in our bones, the essential truth that God himself loves us like crazy and that he's going to do something important in us and through us, that true hope is born. Here's how the Bible puts it: "Let us therefore approach the throne of [God's] grace with boldness, so that we may receive mercy and find grace to help in our time of need" (Hebrews 4:16). God wants us to live confidently, expectantly, and boldly. Dare to hope!

10. Remember Jesus. When it comes to a life of prayer, there's no better teacher and role model than Jesus himself. He didn't just talk about it, he lived it. The Bible describes how he make it his habit to go off and pray. He prayed for guidance. He prayed for strength. He prayed for being centered on God's will. He prayed in order to be prepared for times of testing and rejection. He didn't pray in order to escape from the world; he prayed in order to be ready to change the world.

When Jesus' original followers saw how powerful his prayer life was, they wanted to be like him and pray like him. So they came and asked him to teach them to pray. You can check out the story in Luke 11:1-13. Jesus told them some of the same things we've been saying (don't be a phony; don't make a show out of it; pray for your enemies; be confident; be persistent. And then he taught them a pattern for prayer— what we now call the Lord's Prayer. In the final chapter of this book you'll find a helpful guide to praying the Lord's Prayer for yourself.

One final thought. You may have noticed that many Christians have a habit of praying "in the name of Jesus." Here's why: In a profound way, the Bible presents Jesus as our intercessor, our mediator, our go-between. That means we don't have to stand alone or pray on our own before God. Jesus stands alongside us or goes on ahead before us. This lets us be both humble and bold before God at the same time. The Christian writer Philip Yancey reminds us that Jesus didn't stop praying for his disciples after he ascended to heaven. "In fact, the New Testament's only glimpse of what Jesus is doing right now depicts him at the right hand of God" where he always lives to intercede for us (Hebrews 7:25). Think about that: Jesus himself is busy, right now, remembering you, praying for you, interceding for you. You are not forgotten.

Prayers That Have Made a Difference

When we pray, we welcome God to where we are and what we're going through, and we make room for him in our life. Inmates have told us that the prayers that follow helped them know that God was with them and for them.

Psalm 23

"The 23rd psalm reminds me that God is with me—even when I'm down."

The Lord is my shepherd; I shall not want.

He makes me lie down in green pastures,

he leads me beside quiet waters,

he restores my soul.

He guides me in paths of righteousness

for his name's sake.

Even though I walk

through the valley of the shadow of death,

I will fear no evil,

for you are with me;

your rod and your staff,

they comfort me.

You prepare a table before me

in the presence of my enemies.

You anoint my head with oil;

my cup overflows.

Surely goodness and love will follow me

all the days of my life,

and I will dwell in the house of the Lord

forever.

The Lord's Prayer

This is one of multiple common versions of the prayer from Matthew 6:9-13.

Our Father in heaven,

hallowed be your name,

your kingdom come,

your will be done

on earth as in heaven.

Give us today our daily bread.

Forgive us our debts,

as we also have forgiven our debtors.

And lead us not into temptation,

but deliver us from the evil one.

The Serenity Prayer

"The Serenity Prayer reminds me that the only person I can change is myself."

God, grant me the serenity to accept the things I cannot change,

The courage to change the things I can,

And the wisdom to know the difference.

The Prayer of St. Francis

Lord, make me a channel of thy peace;

that where there is hatred, I may bring love;

that where there is wrong, I may bring the spirit of forgiveness;

that where there is discord, I may bring harmony;

that where there is error, I may bring truth;

that where there is doubt, I may bring faith;

that where there is despair, I may bring hope;

that where there are shadows, I may bring light;

that where there is sadness, I may bring joy.

Lord, grant that I may seek rather to comfort than to be comforted;

to understand, than to be understood;

to love, than to be loved.

For it is by self-forgetting that one finds.

It is by forgiving that one is forgiven.

It is by dying that one awakens to eternal life.

"A Prayer for Those Who Don't Know Christ"

Lord Jesus! You,

Who in the most bitter moments of Your passion

showed an ardent thirst for souls,

grant that we may share in this thirst.

Give us the light to grow

in the knowledge of Your word

and grant us strength so that,

by collaborating in preaching this word

at every moment of our lives,

we may bring to You,

through Your holy Church,

and the intercession of Your holy Mother,

innumerable souls who live far from the truth.

Grant this so that with You,

through You and in You,

they may be reconciled to the Eternal Father,

in union with whom,

together with the Holy Spirit,

You live and reign forever and ever.

The Breastplate of St. Patrick

This prayer helped St. Patrick face oppression, conflict and other challenges. This is only a short piece of the fuller prayer.

I arise today

Through God's strength to pilot me:

God's might to uphold me,

God's wisdom to guide me,

God's eye to look before me,

God's ear to hear me,

God's word to speak for me,

God's hand to guard me,

God's way to lie before me,

God's shield to protect me,

God's host to save me

From snares of devils,

From temptations of vices,

From everyone who shall wish me ill,

Both far and near,

Alone and in multitude.

Christ to shield me today

Against poison, against burning,

Against drowning, against wounding,

So that there may come to me abundance of reward.

Christ with me, Christ before me, Christ behind me,

Christ in me, Christ beneath me, Christ above me,

Christ on my right, Christ on my left,

Christ when I lie down, Christ when I sit down, Christ when I arise,

Christ in the heart of every man who thinks of me,

Christ in the mouth of everyone who speaks of me,

Christ in every eye that sees me,

Christ in every ear that hears me.

I arise today

Through a mighty strength, the invocation of the Trinity,

Through belief in the threeness,

Through confession of the oneness,

Of the Creator of Creation.

I bind myself to the strong Name of the Trinity;

By calling on the Three in One, and One in Three,

Who made everything,

Eternal Father, Spirit, Word:

Praise to the Lord of my salvation,

Salvation is of Christ the Lord.

Praying Your Own Prayers

Every prayer we memorize was once prayed for the first time by someone like you. The following list can help you pray about what you're
thinking about. It helps to be specific in prayer, so as you pray for
comfort for your family, for example, pray about real issues you know
they're facing: difficult neighbors, maybe, or finding a job.

God, please comfort

Me

My family

My friends on the outside

My cell mate

Other inmates who are hurting

People I've hurt

Victims of crime

Victims of accidents

Victims of natural disasters

God, please forgive

Me

People who have wronged me

People who haven't kept their promises to me

Other inmates who have hurt people

God, please provide

For my family's needs

For my case

For my daily needs in prison

For my life after prison

For my day-to-day well-being

God, please help me

With my case

With my relationships

With my adjustment to prison life

God, thank you

For my relationships

For my health

Some people find it helpful to pray the same prayers daily. these prayers are often more general:

In the morning

"God, please help me keep my head up today."

"God, I'll be with you today if you'll be with me."

"God, give me patience and courage, wisdom and strength."

"God, this day is yours."

In the evening

"God, thanks for bringing me through another day."

"God, I trust you with all I saw and heard today."

"God, watch over me as I sleep."

Think About It. Talk About It.

1. Did you pray as a child? If so, who taught you to pray, and what kind of prayers did you pray? If not, have you ever tried to pray as an adult?

2. Do you find prayer

a) natural   b) weird   c) difficult   d) comforting
e) scary   f) powerful   g) other

3. Look back at the prayers that other inmates said helped them know that God was with them and for them. Which of those prayers appeals to you the most right now? Why do you think that is?

4. When it comes to prayer, do you find it difficult to follow the advice to "be persistent and respect God's No"? Do you tend to give up easily? Do you have a hard time accepting No for an answer?

5. Of the top ten things we shared about prayer, which one(s) did you find the most helpful and meaningful?

Walk Like a Christian: 12 Steps Toward Thriving Spiritually

When Christians think about Jesus calling himself "The Way" (see John 14:6) and inviting us to follow him, we're reminded that following him is an *ongoing journey*. Jesus never wanted people to stand still and tip their hat to him. He wants us to be on the move, to walk with him, to walk like him.

But walking with Jesus doesn't come naturally for us. We're used to walking our own way, doing our own thing, heading down our own path. Walking like a Christian—walking like Jesus himself—is a learning process. Just like a child learning to take those first awkward baby steps then slowly walking, then running, learning to walk spiritually is a bumpy process that includes a lot of falling. We need to take it one step at a time to get up to speed following Jesus' way of life.

Speaking of "steps," for over seventy years Alcoholics Anonymous has been engaged in a journey of transformation, one group of people at a time: from deeply-addicted repeat offending to sober living, from insanity to sanity, from broken spirits and broken relationships to restoration, from the terrible isolation of addiction to true community. In A.A., people undergo change by following a 12-step program—a series of steps that are both incredibly practical and incredibly spiritual, incredibly personal and incredibly communal, that are incredibly hard, but that work incredibly well. A.A. isn't a perfect organization, but they've helped a lot of people along the way.

You may be surprised that A.A. has deep Christian roots that go back to the Bible itself. The "step-process" itself can be traced back 500 years to a Catholic saint by the name of Ignatius Loyola and his *Spiritual Exercises*. These roots appear again in the twentieth century, in a group of Christians called the Oxford Group. They believed that God will change us—step by step—and that we need to surrender to God, be honest, be courageous, and be there for one another.

It was these Christians who gave the founders of A.A. their fundamental steps. And then A.A. took this Christian wisdom, tweaked it for alcoholics, added a few extra steps (to close the loopholes!) and worked it, and worked it, and worked it. We offer them as one approach you might want to take. Read them through and see if they ring true for you.

Step One: Humility
We hit bottom. We get clarity. We admit we can't.

We start by admitting that our lives have become unmanageable, that we are powerless over the sin of _____ . Whatever that sin or those sins are for you, *you* make it specific, you fill in the blank.

It's not exactly a fun place to start, is it? Admission—confession—is usually painful and humiliating. It's something we'd rather avoid or deny. A.A. folks say that alcohol has "lashed" them. For many of us, only the bitter experience and the awful consequences of finally hitting bottom put us on the road to change. Why hit bottom? Because half-measures never work.

It's hard and humiliating and shameful for most of us to admit defeat, to confess that we're weak and powerless. Most of us want to think that we're competent, strong, and capable—able to keep things more or less under control. When we hit bottom we finally see for ourselves what's already been clear to the people around us—that no matter what we might say, our self-will just doesn't *work*. And that means we usually have to let go of some powerful voices inside ourselves. Like the voice that says, "If you want it badly enough, you'll get it." Or the voice that says, "If you just try hard enough, you can manage it." Or the voice that says, "Relax, everything you need is already inside yourself."

Step one says, "Those voices are lies," and that St. Paul was right when he wrote,

> I'm at the end of my rope. I can't do it. Can't cope. Can't manage. Can't do the good I want to. And can't stop doing the evil I don't want to. I can't free myself from my old, sinful self. Wretched man that I am! (Check out Romans 7:14-25.)

Step one is humbling, and it demands honesty. Honesty can be painful and shameful because it strips away all those protective layers of myth and denial and phoniness that we wrap ourselves in. Honesty shows us for the weak, selfish, out-of-control drunks, addicts, perverts, critics, liars and phonies that we've become. Step one leaves us feeling naked and exposed. No cover. That means no excuses and no false hopes.

But thank God for step one, because without it we'd never get to step two.

Step Two: Hope
We begin to trust that God could restore us.

If step one strips away our false confidence, then step two offers true hope in return. Step two says that "we came to believe that God, a power greater than ourselves, could restore us to sanity." We step from hopelessness to hope, from despair in ourselves to hope in God.

Step two says, "Stop despairing and start daring to hope." Dare to remember that God's not only *there*, but there *for us—powerfully*. So *who* do we hope for? We hope for Jesus, the Deliverer, the one who comes in power to set us free. *What* do we hope for? At A.A., it's that God "could restore us to sanity." For Christians, it's what the Bible calls salvation— wholeness, freedom, joy, abundant life.

Hope usually gets born in us when God works through the testimony and encouragement of others. Listen carefully here: Hope just has to get born in us. It doesn't have to be perfect. At this stage, hope just has to be able to say one thing: "I couldn't, but God could." And with that, we take the next step.

Step Three: Surrender
We stop procrastinating. We decide. We start turning it over to God.

We make a decision to turn our will and our lives over to the care of God. In step three we finally stop procrastinating. We stop saying, "Of course I want to change, but just not quite yet." In step three we make a *decision,* a conscious and deliberate step.

At this point, it becomes a matter of the *will.* Consequences can force us to hit bottom. Consequences can force a nasty wake-up call *against our will.* But consequences can't ever force us, against our will, to take this step of surrender. We have to take this step *with our will.*

We're standing at the door to a whole new way of life; do we have the *willingness* to turn the handle and step through? Are we ready to renounce our independence and make a declaration of dependence on God? Are we ready to stop playing God—and let God be God? Are we ready to turn over not just that one problem area that's giving us fits but our very will and our whole life? Are we ready to take down all those "off limits" signs that we post for God? Because if we're not, then we're still back at step one—we're still pursuing the fantasy of being in control.

Step three asks us if we are ready to surrender, to risk it all, to trust, to hand over our will and our lives—and open ourselves up to becoming what St. Paul calls a living sacrifice (Romans 12:1). Are we ready to surrender not once, but a thousand times a day? Are we ready to let God's hands hold the controls, day and night—today, tomorrow and forever?

This is true spirituality—a raw, gritty, life-or-death business, finding

God's will and aligning ours with his, asking God to relieve us from our bondage to ourselves. This is true spirituality—to really say and pray in every situation, "Not my will, Lord, but your will be done." We take this step by soaking ourselves in the truth of God's Word, personally searching our own hearts in prayer, and leaning on others who are on the same path.

Step Four: Courage

We go deeper. We step up to the mirror. We face ourselves. We take inventory. We clean house.

We make a "searching and fearless moral inventory of ourselves." The guys who started A.A. were businessmen, so they understood the importance of taking inventory. They said that there's a huge difference between what you think you have and what you really have. They said sometimes the only thing you can do is get down into the basement and check the merchandise, piece by piece. *What's here? What's missing? What's good? What's spoiled?*

Step four means no more fooling ourselves. No more vagueness. We step on a spiritual scale and see what it says. Step four means getting specific and doing some moral bookkeeping, some thorough spiritual housecleaning. It means sweeping a high-powered searchlight over our whole moral life: our thoughts, our feelings, our attitudes, our behaviors, our history with God and others.

It's a pretty scary proposition, isn't it? It means digging around down inside—down in the stuff we try to repress and would like to forget. That's why it needs to be fearless, because we have to push through the scariness of the nasty stuff that has built up.

> My "stuff" includes what I find so very ugly in others—jealousy, the need to be right, using people.
> —Dan

How do we do a moral inventory? One way would be to use a kind of moral checklist. The key is to learn to ask the deep, probing questions. Try working with what the folks at A.A. call "the grudge list."

Lots of us have found that it's our *resentments* that most often keep us from God. Try asking yourself, "Who and what do I resent? And why?" Be honest. Figure out where you feel you've been sinned against and where you need to forgive. Then move on to where you've sinned (whose grudge list you're probably on), and where you need to seek and ask for forgiveness. Where and when have you gone wrong? How and why have you messed up and fallen short?

Centuries of experience teach that we need to get this kind of thing down on paper so that we can look at it objectively. And experience also teaches that this step takes time to process. It might take a month to work it out and write it down. That's okay. You've got time, right?

For most of us, this whole idea is both appealing and terrifying. Some of us are thinking, "Oh great! I already feel horrible about myself. Now I get to pile on even more." Those of us who tend toward being self-justifying are probably going to resent the claim that we all have serious house-cleaning to do. They will look at their grudge list and think, "Hey, look! If anything, *it's these other people* who really need to do a serious moral inventory, not me!"

But in the end, each of us has to walk our own Christian walk. The moral inventory is *ours*, not someone else's. That means the pain and the guilt are ours. But it also means that the insight and potential for change that the inventory stirs up are ours as well.

It takes courage to step into the basement of our heart and take stock of what's really there. It takes courage to face up to ourselves. And the Bible tells us that courage is a gift from the Holy Spirit. So ask the Holy Spirit to give you the courage you need for this step and for the steps to come.

Step Five: Confession

We go face-to-face with God and someone else. We practice humility. We join the community of forgiven sinners. We surrender our secrets. We hear the words of forgiveness. We feel free and cleansed.

The fifth step says that we "admit to God, to ourselves, and to another human being the exact nature of our wrong." It doesn't take a genius to figure out where the sticking point is here, does it? *Admit . . . to another human being . . . the exact nature of our wrong.*

The question is inevitable; we're all asking it: "Why does someone else have to get involved in this process? Isn't this inventory between me and God? So why can't I do it totally on my own?"

The answer is, because it simply doesn't work on our own. It never has. And it never will. Listen carefully to why this is: Taking a shortcut here and trying to avoid this humbling process just cements us deeper in our problems. It leaves us alone with our secrets, stuck in isolation and loneliness. God's Word says (and experience teaches) that without someone else involved, we'll be stuck with either too much guilt or too much self-justification. Either we'll be *exaggerating* our sins and not hearing the healing word of forgiveness, or else we'll be *excusing* our sins and not hearing the healing word of forgiveness.

In the Bible, the letter of James coaches us to do this:

> Confess your sins to each other, and pray for each other so that you may be healed. (James 5:16)

If we're going to practice true humility, we need each other. We need some practical advice from outside ourselves, because we need to bridge that gap of shame that isolates us. We need someone else to confirm that we really are cleaning house and not just pretending. Most of all, we need to hear someone tell us the words of forgiveness we can't fully tell ourselves.

To do this properly, you need someone you can trust, someone able to understand and to keep confidence. You need someone who won't judge you or gossip about you. You need someone who will reassure you and confirm to you that you're forgiven, even when you just keep condemning yourself. You need someone who can be a "little Christ" to you.

So the question now is, *Do you have that someone in your life?* Because people like that can be hard to find—inside or outside. If you don't have that someone, then that's job number one. And if you do, then you've got a gift that you need to use. Sometimes the greatest spiritual gifts you're ever going to be given are already near you. Ask around. Give it time. God will lead you to that person.

Think About It. Talk About It.

1. How would you fill in the blank in the following sentence? My life has become unmanageable, and I am powerless over the sin of _____ . Now, try saying that out loud to yourself. Is it true? Is it humbling?

2. Do you think that God could deal with the unmanageable things in your life? Why or why not? How does that make you feel?

3. Does it seem depressing, scary, or wonderful (or a combination of all three) to "surrender" yourself to God? Are you ready to stop procrastinating and just turn it over to God (either for the first time, or all over again)?

4. Do you have the courage to look deep inside yourself and see what's missing or spoiled? Do you have a list of resentments that you still need to deal with? Who and what do you resent? And why?

5. Speaking of courage and humility, have you ever truly confessed your secrets and sins to another person? If so, what happened? If not, why not? Ask God to prepare you to take this step.

Steps Six and Seven: Repentance

We get ready. And then we ask. We do an about-face. We turn around. We pivot our will. We make a second and deeper surrender to God.

Steps six and seven say that we "were entirely ready to have God remove all these defects of character," and we "humbly asked him to remove our shortcomings."

This is the turn-around step, the about-face, the step of repentance. It's taking all those sins, shortcomings, and character defects from our inventory, and then not only looking at them, but actually letting go of them.

But here's the cruel irony of sin. *More often than not, it's the things we most hate about ourselves that are the hardest to let go of.* It's amazing how often we define ourselves by our problem areas. I'm hot-headed, crazy, proud and defiant, a drug user, out of control, a risk-taker. We worry about who we would be if those things in us got changed. We wonder, "What will be left of me?"

So let's just be honest and say upfront that almost none of us are *that* ready. Not *entirely* ready. We all have our sticking points—hidden or otherwise. But that's okay, because that's not really the point. Not yet. The point here is, *Are we willing to be willing?* Are we willing to ask God to make a start with those things? And are we humble enough to ask and keep on asking, to simply say, "Lord, I'm willing. Help my unwillingness"? (Check out the story of Jesus and man with a sick son in Mark 9:17-24.) That's the step that we're talking about. It's a willingness to step towards our destiny in Christ, over and over and over again.

In a way, we've circled back to step three: deciding to turn our lives and wills over to God. Only, this time, it's a lot more specific. This time, we're a lot more aware of exactly what we're turning over, and what a real about-face we're asking God to help us make.

We've come seven steps so far. Starting to see the connection yet? Feel the process unfold? This is a journey we're on, a journey to Christlikeness.

Steps Eight and Nine: Restitution

We face our debts. We apologize to those we've harmed. We pay back. We repair damage.

At this point we need to do what we can to get right with other people, to do what we can to repair damaged relationships. We "make a list of persons we have harmed and become willing to make amends to them all," and then we go ahead and "make direct amends to such people whenever possible, except when to do so would injure them or others."

We'd love to be completely free at this stage, but we aren't. We're still carrying a lot of baggage from our past. We have to ask ourselves, "Who do we owe and what do we owe them?"

It's a great question that we don't like to ask ourselves. The very idea of owing somebody—of being indebted, of having things unresolved and unpaid, of having some obligation out there *with our name on it*, just waiting for us—makes us feel anything but free. And at our core, we just want to be free, right? Debt-free. Obligation free. Free.

But if we don't take this two-part step and deal with this question head on, we'll never be free. We'll continue to have an uneasy conscience. We'll continue avoiding eye contact with certain people. We'll continue to be saddled with those lingering debts out there that weigh us down in here.

But before you come up with a snap answer about who you owe, think about this first. Think about how Jesus calls us to radical, sacrificial love, and to a deep and life-long obligation to one another. How are you doing on *that* scorecard? If we measure where we are and what we owe not by our own self-serving standards but by the standards that Jesus sets for us, then we're debtors, plain and simple. All of us. And that's why the daily prayer Jesus taught us includes the phrase "forgive us our *debts* as we forgive our debtors."

Translate the word however you want to: debts, sins, trespasses. Or, how about translating it this way: *damage*. "Forgive us the damage we've done, as we forgive those who have damaged us." We do damage to people both by what we do, deliberately or accidentally, *and also* by what we fail to do—all the damage we inflict by not caring, by shirking our responsibility.

Think about the long trail of damaged people that we each leave behind us in life. We're like a storm blowing through a crowded town. We're like a sick person spreading an infection. Think of all the harsh words, half-truths, and critical comments we've said—as well as all the words of comfort or praise for others that we refuse or fail to say. Think of the damage we do by soaking up all the attention and energy and leaving none for others. Think of the damage we do by withdrawing into our own world and leaving others to fend for themselves. Think of all the damage we've done to our kids by not being there for them.

Think of the damage we do by our selfishness and self-absorption. The damage we do by turning a blind eye to someone in trouble. The damage we do by treating women as objects. The damage we inflict by the ripple effect of our anger, our depression, our alcoholism, our lust, our competitiveness, our judgmentalism, our lack of humor, our laziness, our envy, our greed, our ingratitude.

Think about all the accumulated damage we've done! All that cost! Think about the crowd of faces of people we've damaged.

But then think about this, too—about what we can still do in response. Think about the steps we can still take, the damage we can still repair, the hurts we can still ease, the fences we can still mend, the debts we can still repay, the relationships we can still restore.

Have the courage to take the next step. Think about how you can make amends to that crowd of faces you've damaged. What do you owe them that you are currently in a position to give?

Well, for one thing you owe them *the truth*, an honest admission of what you've done. No excuses. No rationalizations. Just the truth.

You also owe them *an apology*. A simple, heart-felt "I'm sorry." Personal remorse for the damage done. No faking it. No groveling. Just an apology.

You owe them an offer of restitution. Some sort of repayment. Appropriate *payback*. If you've been "a taker" in the past, then start a pattern of giving away. If you've been missing in action, then be interested. If you've been domineering, then listen. If you've been harsh, then be gentle. Of course it's not always easy to figure out what to do in any particular situation. You'll have to use judgment and sensitivity. But payback is a key to rebuilding trust.

You also owe the people you damaged the *evidence of a changed life*. And that's why it's better to "make amends" at steps 8 and 9 instead of steps 2 or 3. People need to see that the change in us is real for them to take our offers of restitution seriously.

And finally, you owe those you've damaged *their right to respond*. This is probably the scariest part of all, because the people you've damaged might keep on grumbling. They might let you have it with both barrels. They might express their ongoing disappointment or disgust—tell you that they hate you and don't want to have anything to do with you. They may very well reject your apology, make unreasonable demands, want revenge and refuse forgiveness. It's possible that the damage may have been too great, too deep. It's possible that other person may be too unforgiving. The painful truth is, we don't get to take the step of full reconciliation. But it's only by taking this step of restitution that the door to reconciliation can ever truly open.

Sometimes we can't make amends with the people we've damaged without creating a whole new round of pain for them. It may be too painful for people we've victimized (or their families) to deal with our desire to make restitution. Instead of repairing the damage, we may be opening up a wound prematurely. We may intend it for good, and desire it for our own growth, but the wound may be too deep, or the time too soon, for someone to offer it. A good rule of thumb in this instance would be to pray carefully, write out what we wish to say, and share it with people we trust for their input and advice.

Steps Ten and Eleven: Persistence and Rededication
We discipline ourselves daily. We buddy up. We keep going. We put one foot in front of the other. We grow one day at a time. We leave nothing out.

We're now at the stage where the dramatic and radical intervention of the earlier steps (big surrender to God, initial moral inventory, grudge lists, the drama of making amends) gives way to the perseverance and daily discipline of doing these things again and again—working the steps, working the manual, exercising what we've learned, drilling in the fundamentals, grooving it into our daily routine. Think of this as the open-ended stage where we're "rehabbing" spiritually. We're at that stage, that phase, where it's all about perseverance and daily discipline.

Steps ten and eleven are about going deeper and deeper into the day-by-day discipline of a changed life, into understanding spiritual change as a life-long exercise, to be worked out and worked on one day at a time. It's now about the daily disciplining of heart and mind—daily work, daily routines, daily check-ups, daily disciplines—so that these things become less and less what we're told to *do* and more and more simply who and how we *are*.

Here's how the A.A. folks put it:

> *Step Ten:* We continued to take personal inventory and when
> we were wrong promptly admitted it.

> *Step Eleven:* We sought through prayer and meditation to
> improve our conscious contact with God, praying only for
> knowledge of his will for us and the power to carry that out.

When you hit step ten in A.A. or one of the other 12-step programs,
something interesting kicks in. You get a kind of worksheet. A daily log.
A checklist. It's similar to that searching and fearless moral inventory of
step 4, only this time it's only for today. You forget the past. You forget
yesterday. And you just focus on today. Just keep it current. Ask yourself
"How did *today* go?"

Here's the underlying idea: *Today nothing should be left out.* Nothing of
who I am should be left out of the process. All that I am, everything
that I've got, it's all part of the mix. No motive unexamined. No behavior unchecked. None of my bad and self-destructive and God-dishonor-
ing habits are going to be allowed to grow back unopposed.

To make sure that nothing gets left out, you find yourself a 10th-step
buddy, an accountability partner who's going through the same thing at
the same time. Just as it's easier to clean house when you're doing it with
someone else, it's easier to do your ongoing spiritual house-cleaning
with someone else. Because buddy systems work. Because God made us
to encourage each other

We're talking about spiritual "growth." Not perfection. *Growth.* A.A.
calls it "*improving our conscious contact with God.*" We call it growing
closer in our relationship with God, going deeper and becoming more

174

disciplined in our prayer life, being transformed and growing into the image of Christ. In one place, the Bible puts it this way:

> May you be filled with the knowledge of God's will in all spiritual wisdom and understanding, so that you may lead lives worthy of the Lord, fully pleasing to him, as you bear fruit in every good work and as you grow in the knowledge of God. (Colossians 3:16)

It's about the growth process of being filled, of growing, of bearing fruit. And so the point of moving on to steps 10 and 11 is to move from the crisis of the intervention stage to rehab and renewal and restoration. It's to move from damage control to some new construction, from emptiness to fulfillment, from decay to growth, from powerlessness to empowerment, and leaving nothing out in the process. It's about just living the Christian life one day at a time, walking the Christian walk, just putting one foot in front of the other.

Instead of constantly bouncing off the walls, this is where we get grounded. This is where the lessons take deep root, where the insights get put into action, where we get empowered, where nothing gets left out and everything gets engaged. This is where we're finally in position to take the final step.

Step Twelve: Mission
We carry the message. We give it away. We pass it on. We give ourselves in love. We leave no one behind.

We've now come eleven steps towards a changed life in God. Each step building on the last. Each step intensifying the transformation. Each step growing in power. Eleven steps of accumulated power and insight and truth and freedom. Eleven steps to concentrate spiritual change. And then one final step to unleash its power for others. One step to channel it outwards.

This final step is about taking that life-changing gift of God and doing the only appropriate thing we can do—letting it flow through us. Giving it away.

Give it to *whom?* To whomever needs it.

Give it *why?* Because there's no greater need, no greater joy, and no higher purpose in life.

Give it *how?* As effectively and lovingly as we can.

Give it *where and when?* Wherever and whenever it's needed.

A.A.'s step 12 says,

> Having had a spiritual awakening as a result of these steps, we tried to carry this message to alcoholics, and to practice these principles in all our affairs.

They call it "carrying the message." We call it *evangelism.* Either way, it's the same thing. Either way, it's not about "imposing" anything. It's about *intervening* with love in the lives of people who are suffering. This step is all about making sure that no one is left out of the loop, out of the healing process, out of the community of changed lives.

This is the step that Jesus gave to his followers after he taught them to walk in his footsteps. He promised them that they would not only do what he did, but that they would do even greater things. He commissioned, commanded, and released them into the whole world, for the sake of the whole world—to heal it, repair it, and love it. He built them up, and then he sent them in the power of his love, so that no one would be left out, and so that all might be his disciples—living in his way, empowered by his Spirit, transformed and liberated from the inside out. "*Go, make disciples*," he said. Go and be in the life-changing business.

Jesus teaches us to keep looking for opportunities, but not to rush people. Step in when there's an opening and receptivity, but don't chase those who don't want to change. Do everything out of love, but don't be afraid to stir up the waters in someone's life, because God uses that to get us all to step one. Don't look down on anyone else, but don't ever forget that all of us are sinners and lost and hurting. Remember to offer friendship and fellowship, but don't ever turn this into something that somebody owes you. Don't force anyone. But make sure that no one is left out or left behind.

Make step twelve your own personal mission, but don't try to do this on your own. When Jesus was training his first disciples to go and carry his message, he sent them out two by two. So team up with others and go where someone needs you, when someone needs you, and do whatever it takes to get them through that rough patch. This isn't "imposing your religion" on anybody. This is *love*. At its best, at its purest, at its deepest, it's nothing less than God's incredible and undeserved and life-changing love flowing through us and touching others.

Imagine the joy and the satisfaction of being used like that. Imagine that as a picture of the power of God's transforming love that might flow through us in the prison you're sitting in. Imagine the greater things yet to be done through us. Imagine what God could do with us. Imagine how pleased God would be with us. With eleven steps we get changed. With twelve steps the *whole world* gets changed.

So keep on walking. Keep on walking like a Christian. Keep on walking like our Lord. Keep on walking to our Lord. Because God's not nearly done with us yet. Keep on walking. God's got some surprises up ahead. After all, you still have time.

Think About It. Talk About It.

1. What are those character defects that you know you have, but you still find hard to let go of? Are you at the stage where you're willing to let God help you with that?

2. How hard would it be for you to make a list of the people you've damaged by what you've done or by what you've failed to do? Could you begin to repair the damage by offering others an apology, payback, evidence of a changed life, or their right to respond?

3. Are you ready to take the step of dedicating yourself to God and leading a changed life on a daily basis?

4. Does it feel exciting to think that God has a mission for you, that God can make you more Christ-like, and that God's love might flow through you to help change another person's life for the better? Does that inspire you to keep going to the next step?

5. As you look over the twleve steps to lasting change, what step are you at today? Do you feel ready and eager to move on to the next one?

From Where I Sit: Dan, Former Inmate

Dan was initially processed through the Northern Reception Center and then was sent to do his time in Lincoln Correctional in downstate Illinois. He wrote this longer reflection on surviving spiritually just days after his release. We thought it was worth sharing the whole thing with you.

When I first arrived in receiving, I couldn't believe what my life had come to. I felt like a failure and couldn't understand how a person who cared about his family and friends, who wanted to succeed in life, could wind up in prison.

While in receiving I began to think of why my life had gone the way it had. The more I thought about it, the more angry I became. I wasn't treated badly by family or friends, but why had God let me down? I'd asked him to help me and it seemed that all those prayers went unheard or unanswered. The more I thought about it, the angrier I became. After all, isn't God supposed to help people who ask for his help?

I began to wonder if I had something to do with the way my life had gone. When I started to get honest with myself, I began to see that I'd lived a lifestyle with myself at the center. My needs and desires came before anyone else's. I was forever worried about my pleasure. I used alcohol and drugs to cope with a world that I thought had somehow forgotten me. When I was able to really start getting honest, I began to see that I'd never given the straight world a chance. I'd always assumed that the people who put lots of time and energy into family, work, and school somehow didn't want me around. I was pretty surprised to finally see that it was me who didn't give the world a chance, not the other way around.

After I realized this fact, I saw that I had an opportunity to either prepare myself for life or sink into my old negative attitudes. We all know that in prison we can stand around the deck talking about women, drugs, "the game," or we can focus our energies on positive things. I asked God to help me work at building an attitude towards life that worked. In prison I began to involve myself in AA and school. I stopped glamorizing drug and alcohol abuse.

I started to discover that the more energy I put into the positive, the more I could respect myself and the better I felt.

Lots of times I'd get a bit discouraged. I'd think, "Well, now since I know better and want to be on a positive road, people like these guards should treat me with respect." I found out that just because I'm doing the right thing, it doesn't mean that others will be on the same page.

I also found out—and am constantly learning—that everything takes time and patience. It took me many years to mess up my life, and it's going to take some time before people trust me. It's going to take time and hard work to "get a life" that works on a healthy level. I found out that just like in the free world, I can make choices while I'm in prison that will positively affect my life. I would always hear other inmates say stuff like, "I act this way 'cause I'm in prison and I can't let people think I'm a punk." When I have that kind of attitude, nothing is going to change. I need to rise above that prison atmosphere and do what I know to be right. At the end of the day, I have to live with myself and my actions. At the end of the day I want to lie down with some peace and the knowledge that I really did my best today.

There are so many ways to begin a new life in prison. Like I said, I started going to school and got involved in AA. I read my Bible. I stopped watching negative TV shows (my mind is already negative enough from the lifestyle I lived). Another thing I decided to do was to not complain to my family or friends when I called home or wrote letters. They were worried enough about me without me telling them even more troublesome stuff on the phone.

I stopped arguing with other inmates. When I'd hear a conversation start to heat up, I'd get away from it. I stopped hanging out with people who I knew weren't ready for a positive change yet. I made a conscious decision to be one of those people we sometimes meet in prison who are really trying to do the right things. Some of these things I did because I just knew they were the right way to new life, and some I learned in AA, from the Bible, or from other positive activities I was involved in.

I don't want to give anyone the idea that any of this came easily or naturally to me. It takes lots of practice, and I'll be learning for the rest of my life. But as soon as I made the real decision to seriously change my life, I began to get the benefits.

I saw lots of inmates act a certain way in church and another way on the deck. I made a commitment to myself to behave in a certain way whether I was alone in my cell, on the deck, in the chow hall, at church, or AA. I told myself, "This new life is for me—now, today! This isn't some sneaky way to gain favor with God today so I can do what I want tomorrow. I need to make a clear choice in what I say, do, read, how I treat others—so I can be free!"

I know all about the prisons of addiction, hate, fear, prejudice, and a life without purpose. I know all about the physical prison of the penitentiary. With the help of God I can begin to rise above these and be a new person with new hopes and dreams. I really can be one of those people that I've always been jealous of because they seem to "get along with life." I no longer need to be an outsider just trying to survive. I can live in happiness and with purpose.

It's important that I have enough faith to believe the people around me who have gone before me. It's important that I choose the right people to be around. Today I choose to be around people who are happy and getting a kick out of the important things in life. People who place real value on peace, health, and helping others. When I hang with people who really want to do the right thing, it makes living right a reality, not just something I've read about.

What I'm constantly reminded of is that this change towards wanting a better life is really a commitment to myself and to God. It doesn't matter what the guys on my wing think. It matters what I think. I'm the one who has to live with me. Also, I need to remember that all this is going to take time. With some issues, it's going to take years of retraining my thought-process to see life differently. I can't get discouraged to the point where I want to give up. God works through people, and when I hang with people who are on the right path, all sorts of doors begin to open.

Inmates Share a Month's Worth of Spiritual Advice

In addition to those great little daily devotional guides that the prison volunteers bring around (like *Our Daily Bread*), we thought you might appreciate 31 daily slices of spiritual advice served up by your fellow inmates. We hope you find them helpful.

"Have faith in God. Have patience and never give up. Just stay focused on the Lord. He knows you want to go home. Just study his Word so that you're ready when you go home."

"If you're surrounded by spiritual people, you'll be a spiritual person. If you're surrounded by negative people, you'll be negative. Whatever you're surrounded by is normal to you. If you get your head right, you won't falter."

"Fellowship is important. Don't force your burden on others."

"Think about what's happened in the penitentiary in the past; there's lots of evil, lots of spiritual warfare in this place. The penitentiary mentality is depressed and angry. Watch the conduct of people before you trust them. Example is important. People aren't perfect; but are they willing to change?"

"You need to do what's best for yourself. It's life and death now."

"What's phony is easy to notice. When a person's heart is not in it, you're not going to see change. We're not going to be able to use God to get out, but God is going to cultivate the gifts he wants to call out in us."

"I've got all the time in the world to get two things straight: to get to know who I really am, and to get to know my Maker. So, who are you? I'm not asking what you did or what you do. You've got this X on your back now; but it's not the end of the world. Nelson Mandela, Malcolm X, the apostle Paul—all were prisoners who accomplished great things. Every man's drama is his drama. The story of Joseph is beautiful for people in prison—especially those who are falsely accused. Don't get lost in "why" you're here; focus on "while" you're here. Even though you're doing time, it's not wasted time. God has inside men."

"Pray today—and every day—for your own family as well for the victim's family."

"What God asks is easy; what life asks is hard. You make one choice, and then a whole range of choices are made for you. I adapted to things I should be terrified by. How about you?"

"People here act like they're afraid to say I love you. New inmates need to know that somebody loves them; it's going to be all right. This is not the time to put your head down; it's time to keep your head up. Take your time; relax; notice what God is doing. Let each other know you love them. Take advantage of all the programs available to you. There's still hope here."

"Chaplains can only do so much, and there are only so many of them. Teachers and volunteers only have so much time and access. Christians in here need to step up. A prayer: 'Lord, give me the strength and wisdom to lead your people.'"

"It's a correctional facility—it's supposed to be corrective—but there's not really a system in place. But I've got an angel in my cell. God is watching over us."

"Be honest and upfront with your celly. Find the common goal of coexisting. Set aside pride, defensiveness, and aggressiveness. You can't maintain your walls forever. The biggest obstacle in prison is the spirit of pride. The strongest mantle a man can have in or out of prison is humility."

"Prison is no place for hypocrisy. Neither is church. You can think you've got something, but not have it. You have to get your mind back. We have two voices—the 'old man' and the Holy Spirit. One has to die. Watch for life change and hypocrisy in the people you meet here; listen to your spirit; train your ear."

"The main things to keep in mind as you live as a Christian are to pay attention to what's going on, to live differently from how other people are living, to answer questions that people ask you, to reach out to and encourage people whenever you can, and to point people toward the cross. The Christian journey in prison is like a wilderness: we were slaves, we're liberated by Christ onto an unknown path; the cross empties us of all our props, and then Jesus leads us through the wilderness into life with God and freedom in Christ."

"Basically, it's better to do your time with Jesus than not. Turn your cell and time into a university. Don't get so caught up in the prison gossip, and pointless TV shows."

"Strive to have a truthful relationship with God. It takes time and discipline to want the relationship. God will give you blessings that you would never believe possible. And in turn, your other relationships will thrive as well."

"The legal system is a long and slow process. There are two things a long-timer has to have: faith and a strong prayer life. There are going to be a lot of matters that will go on outside these walls with your family that you will not be able to help them with personally. This is where your prayer life will help a lot."

"Take one day at a time and don't focus on the things you can't do. Check out these Bible passages today: Isaiah 26:3; John 14:1- 27; Philippians 4:6-7."

"This is Jesus' boot camp. My education made my cell get bigger; my perspective was elevated by the grace of God."

"Could you pray for others today? Basically, when I pray for others throughout the world, it has been meaningful to me. I pray for people that I don't know, things that I see in the news because maybe nobody has prayed for them. It makes a difference for me because I'm able to see what's going on in the world and it keeps me from feeling sorry for myself and my own situation. There are so many people who need God desperately, and I feel for them because they may not even know that they need him."

"People here are skeptics—regardless of what comes out of your mouth, they're watching your footprints. The first thing we do here is evaluate each other. This place is about punishment, not rehabilitation. Ultimately, you're responsible for seeing to your own rehabilitation. Humility is hard for people who have lived their whole lives with their dukes up."

"There are four kinds of people: Sandpaper people—they rub you the wrong way. (Stay put! They help you deal with your ego.) The bug—he's crazy, doesn't care about himself or anything else. (Get away!) The other brother—he smiles to your face but stabs you in the back. (Be yourself! Bear your cross! Allow them to be themselves.) The mentor—he wants you to be better and do better. (Be like a sponge!) So keep looking and watching to determine who you can trust. It's not a weak thing to ask to be removed from a bad situation; that's the act of a wise man."

"Make your prayer simple today: God, I surrender my life to you. Please guide me in the direction you see fit, and give me your grace and mercy along the way."

"Keep crying out to God and each day expect an answer. And know that you are 'more than a conqueror in Christ Jesus' (Romans 8:37)."

"Have faith in Jesus Christ—not in the courts, and most certainly not in Man. Try reading Psalm 23 today."

"Hear this promise from God's Word: 'Be strong and courageous. Do not be afraid or terrified of your enemies, for the Lord your God goes with you. He will never leave you nor forsake you' (Deuteronomy 31:6)."

"With all humility: Son, if you don't change, your out-date will."

"Put your mind on God and watch how the sentence won't affect you at all."

"Now would be the time to consider why you are here. Where did you go wrong? Where are you going on this journey called life? And most importantly, who are you going to allow to be your teacher now? Who is going to be that influence in your life? Who can straighten out this mess you have made of our life? And who can make your wrongs right and put you back on that narrow path? I know from personal experience that if you seek God's guidance you'll find that he will lead you to himself."

"Pray, son! And look at this as an adventure, as a learning opportunity (like college). Learn how not to waste your time. This, too, is a part of your life. Remember that the Bible is evidence that God has a heart for the prisoner: Joseph, Moses, John, Peter, Paul, and even Jesus were imprisoned. And Jesus served the death penalty for us all. Make the most of your time by learning: first, who you are, then who you were, and then who you want to be."

"Prison is full of Bibles and other religious literature. What's often hard to find are Christians or at least other men who are truly interested in a real and positive change. Most inmates seem to feel that change (both inner and outer) can only happen in the free world. They say, 'When I get out I'll be honest, responsible, sober, kind, and help others. But while I'm in prison I have to keep this tough exterior.' What I need, and probably others feel this way too, is a group of inmates that supports real change and admires goodness. In here, lots of guys go to chapel and Bible study but continue to live the life of an inmate. I know that faith and change need to begin now, here, for me to have a chance on the outside."

"Time in my own mind came to be a thing that I sometimes dreaded. I never knew exactly how to deal with the shame, self-loathing and anger that I sometimes felt. Prison is hard, but my thoughts in prison were much more difficult to deal with than the physical surroundings or other inmates. I found out that much of the time, in or out of prison, I'm the problem. I often want to blame situations or people, but it's how I deal with life that makes or breaks me. And how I deal with life depends entirely on what my relationship to God is. How about you?"

"When I've been putting real time and thought into my relationship with God my life has a certain natural flow to it. When I neglect my relationship to God I find myself living in a sort of low-level but constant indefinable fear. This fear causes all kinds of other negativity like anger and mistrust. It's up to me to keep my relationship with him fresh and close. He's the constant while I'm the variable. He's always there waiting for me to come back to him. And he's waiting for you, too."

"Heavenly Father, I come to you in the name of Jesus. Your Word promises that whoever calls on your name shall be saved. I'm calling on you now. Lord, come into my life and be my Lord and be master over it. I let go of my old ways and give myself to you now. I proudly confess you as my living and powerful Lord. I know that I am now reborn, that I am your beloved son. Move in me in the days ahead so that I can finally grow up into being the man you want me to be. I pray in your holy and powerful name. Amen."

7

SURVIVING SPIRITUALLY BEYOND PRISON

They call it "re-entry" these days. It sounds a little cold and clinical at first, but when you think about it a bit more, it's actually a pretty good term. It reminds us that returning to the outside after time in prison is like a spacecraft coming back to earth.

You may have heard that the "re-entry" phase is actually the most dangerous part of the whole process of space flight. Lots of things can go wrong for a spacecraft coming back into the atmosphere. It can come in too fast and burn up. It can miscalculate and crash land. What's needed is a carefully thought-out plan—a safe glide path back home for a safe landing.

It's no different for an inmate re-entering the outside world. After being locked up for a while, we're no longer adjusted to the outside atmosphere. We can foolishly take things too quickly or too impulsively and simply crash and burn. What we need is a carefully thought-out (and prayed-over) plan to create a safe glide path for ourselves in our first six months after release.

That's what we need, but that's not what we always do. Take a listen to what happened to Dan when he got out.

"What Happened When I Got Out": Dan's Story

About six months before I went home it occurred to me that I really was going home. I became very anxious. Everything started bothering me. Inmates were driving me nuts. I found new hatred for the guards. Standing in chow lines made my heart pound. And if I couldn't get on the phone when I wanted to, I about lost my mind. The funny thing was that I knew all of these attitudes were my problem. I knew nothing had changed with my surroundings; something must have changed in me. I knew I had short timer's disease.

I took some action. I prayed about it—going so far as to pray for the inmates and guards I was getting angry at. I talked about it in my recovery meetings and with fellow believers. These things helped but didn't seem to take it away. About five minutes after I woke up each day my brain would start with the anxiety and resentment.

It was so surprising to me to feel so stressed about going home. I felt more stressed about leaving than I did about coming to prison!

For a long time it had been easier for me to focus on daily prison life. I really didn't want to think about the family, women, and friends that I'd left behind. That was just too painful for me. To me, leaving prison was going to be the end of all my problems. I pictured a warm welcome from family, old friends, past girlfriends. I figured that someone would give me a job. In prison I did lots of working out so my physical health was good. Most importantly, in prison I'd prayed, read the Bible, and was involved in a 12 Step program. I really believed that going home would be like going to Disneyland. No more crazy inmates, guards, staff. No more "celly problems." No more waiting for money in the mail or commissary. I was going to actually be free! In my deepest heart, I believed that my transition would be filled with stress-free laughter and goodwill from the world. Nothing could have been further from the truth.

Prayer definitely helped during this time. So did talking with fellow believers—people I could trust. They advised that I continue to pray, read the Bible and find others to help, even if helping meant nothing more than a short, kind word or deed.

On the way home I got car sick. I hadn't been in a car for years and the motion made me ill. As soon as I arrived at my parents' house I was filled with a sense of guilt and shame. I didn't know exactly what to do next. All of the bright colors of everyday life in the real world sort of scared me. Right away I felt like I didn't fit.

Some good friends came by—friends who are sober and walking a spiritual path. I knew they'd understand just what I was going through. They didn't. How could they—they'd never been to prison for years like I just had. They were a bit confused as to why I seemed so uptight. I tried to explain but was not sure myself. I mean, "Wow, I'm actually home. So why do I feel so weird and afraid?"

I was honest with everyone. I told my friends and family that being home was like being in some alien landscape. That I didn't know what to do with my hands. After a few days I began to notice people sort of losing interest in the novelty of Dan being home. I wanted to call everyone and say, "Hey, don't lose interest. I'm home now and want to be part of life!" People just got on with their lives, and I felt alone and afraid. I literally didn't know what I should be doing every day.

I had a basic understanding that I needed to continue my sobriety through spiritual channels. To me that meant daily prayer, Bible reading, AA, and basic "golden rule" living. I did some of that, but to be honest I did a lot more worrying about what people thought about me and where I was going to find a job. My relationship with God quickly went on the back burner.

I kept saying to myself, "Look what you've done with your life! How will you ever repair it? How will you ever get a job? And what's up with my girl? She seems to be acting weird." It was like at every turn, I felt more and more out of place. Even those old friends seemed unsure about what to say to me. It felt like the world had a secret it wouldn't let me in on. I began to unravel.

We all want to feel connected with God and people. There's nothing worse than feeling alone. After a few weeks home I felt more alone than when I was in prison. My friends in recovery were busy with family, work and school. At church I felt little in common with these good people. I know the pastor says they don't judge, but who doesn't judge? Are there people who really don't judge? So down I went.

In hindsight I missed the turn when I began to care more about what people thought about me than what I was actually doing in my life. My focus became about what I thought others were thinking about me—rather than just doing my very best to do the next right thing. My mind ran round and round, and I forgot the lessons that had been beaten into me by life, prison, and my search for God. I was back to relying on my own broken thinking.

After a serious relapse I knew I had to find a way to really stay on track. Lots of us have gotten on the path many times. The real deal is to stay on it when the going gets tough and uncertain. I moved into a halfway house. I began to see that my troubles are about me and not about how the world treated me. I saw that I need to put real effort into getting positive results if I wanted any. For most of my life I'd found ways of manipulating people to build the life that I wanted. I was always more interested in looking good than doing good. I saw that attitude had to stop.

What happened to Dan is a great example of the complicated challenges of re-entry, and how tough it can be for many of us to survive spiritually on the outside. It isn't just Dan's story; nearly all of us have a similar story dealing with our own case of "short-timer's disease," unrealistic expectations, a lack of careful planning and communication, the awkward experience to adapting to life on the outside, and the sobering realization that life is wonderful, but hard.

Hope and Realistic Expectations

Every inmate who's going home needs *both* profound hope *and* realistic expectations. One of them isn't enough. That's because neither one on its own is going to help us thrive spiritually after prison. Hope without realistic expectations quickly turns into wishful thinking, followed by bitter disappointment. And realistic expectations without deep and profound hope quickly turns into self-fulfilling pessimism and a trip back to prison.

Several years ago Fred was at Stateville Prison leading a small group of men, soon to be released, who were taking a "How to Get and Keep a Job" workshop. Men were busy writing resumes, filling out sample job applications, and learning the dos and don'ts of job interviewing. And in the middle of the training, one of the young men started complaining,

> This is stupid. It's pointless. All these guys are talking so big about getting a job. They're not gonna get a job. They're gonna hit the same streets they came from and start doing the same old things. They'll just be back in here in six months.

When he was asked, "Well, what about you? What makes you different?" he said, "Nothing. I'm no different. I'll be back in here, right along with them."

"But you have some skills, some experience. Why wouldn't you get a job?"

He pulled up his sleeves to reveal tattoos on the inside of his lower arms—tattoos of gangsters with huge smoking guns. And then he said, "Would you hire me, looking like this? Be honest, would you let your daughter date me?"

"I might," I told him, "But couldn't you have them removed? Or wear long sleeves?"

He just looked at me and shrugged. That young man had what he thought were "realistic" expectations, but he had absolutely no hope that things might be different for him. And without hope, he saw no reason to try to do even the little things that might improve his odds. He had fallen deeply into self-fulfilling pessimism. He had literally made himself a "marked man" and told himself that there was no future for him. Because he had no expectation that God would make a way for him, he was busy writing his one-way ticket back into the penitentiary.

What that young man needed most was hope—God's own hope. True hope is God's gift to us. It's based on God's promises to us for a transformed tomorrow. It's a vision of a brighter future planted by God himself deep in our imaginations. True hope comes from God and is based on his own unshakable promises. It isn't just our own self-manufactured optimism based on our own wishful thinking. We asked some inmates whether or not they felt hopeful about surviving spiritually after re-entry. Here's what they told us.

Without a shadow of a doubt—if God is for us, who can be against us! Romans 8:31.
　　　—Jacques

I know God wants good things to happen that I may be blessed, and I can do all things through Christ Jesus who strengthens me!
　　　—JT

As long as God is with me, I will never have any worries! Anymore!!! My life is his now and I will do whatever, go wherever he leads me in my earthly journey that I have left on the planet!
　　　—James

I do feel hopeful because if God gives me the opportunity to come home, I know that he will give me the strength to overcome all that I worry about and fears that I have. He will give me victory over everything that will lead me away from him.
　　　—Anonymous

I know it's God's will for me to help others. Long as I do things God's way I can't go wrong.
　　　—Volney

I feel very hopeful. The Lord has molded me into what he wants me to be. I am prepared to face the trying times after being released from prison. One thing I have learned is patience. With patience I can persevere through the roadblocks that lie ahead.
—Doaikah

Yes, I do because God is my Lord and master, and in him I will continue to serve. I also have a lot of support from family and friends—and I know my weaknesses, and I will stay away from them.
—Robert

Sometimes I do because when I get out I don't want to live on the street. I want to go back to school, have a job. A wife and kids. Will somebody care about me? I'm only being honest.
—Timothy

Yes, because the base of faith is hope.
—Earl

Yeah, I'm counting on God and his promises. So far, after nineteen years, he's kept me. I know he'll have me in his hands.
—Jose

These guys weren't just filled with a profound hope about what would happen to them after prison. After years of growing in their faith inside, they were also excited about how God might put them to good use when they re-enter society. And so we asked them, "What excites you most about the idea of surviving spiritually after prison?" Here's a sampling of what they told us.

What excites me? Coming back to a newness of life. Showing the people who knew me back then how my God has changed my life and has given me a new and better perspective of life and a purpose.
    —Jacques

"God can!" Nelson Mandela, president of South Africa, said that after 27 years in prison at the time apartheid ruled. Trust the Word, remember what and where it brought you from, and dare to dream where it can take you.
    —Anthony

Being an active member within the Body of Christ Jesus, which also helps others identify who God is, and maybe avoid prison and enjoy freedom too.
    —JT

I believe that God has blessed me with a powerful testimony that he wants me to share with others. I know that I can't go out to the same things because now I've experienced every aspect of the gang life and I can share this with others to lead them to Christ and hope that others learn from my mistakes.
    —Anonymous

What excites me most is the thought that I can fulfill God's calling to preach his Word to all corners of the earth, as well as to testify to others about what God has done in my life. I will be given the chance to work with young people who have made some of the choices I have made in my life and offer them a relationship with Christ.
    —Doaikah

To be able to worship with my family in the same church. To be able to minister to others and hopefully inspire others to stay out of drugs and alcohol and trouble.
—Robert

That I can work for God and be a blessing to others and teach his Word all over the world.
—Timothy

To express and tell others about the goodness, mercy, and grace of God. To be sold out for Christ and win others to Christ.
—Jose

My testimony excites me because I know it will save many lives and stop a lot of people from stopping here.
—Rodney

To know what I know now and having the opportunity to be an example to my family and show them that they can do it as well. Being a model to young kids, to share my story of survival, to help those in need spiritually and use the Word as the sword that it is. And to know that without God I wouldn't know my purpose in life, that is to serve the Lord.
—Wilfredo

These kinds of things sound good, of course, but are they realistic? Do they overlook the challenges and difficulties of surviving spiritually after prison? So we went ahead and asked a follow-up question: "Okay, now what worries you most about surviving spiritually after prison?"

I wouldn't say "a worry" but a concern: not being effective in service for the Lord, not accomplishing his purpose, his will for my life.
  —Jacques

Not having an "after prison."
  —Anthony

That I too may find myself forgetting how he's blessed me and begin to doubt and become callous towards others.
  —JT

I worry that I may still be holding back with my witnessing and falling into the temptations that will come my way, that I won't give 100 percent like I should.
  —Anonymous

Dealing with people who don't care about helping me.
  —Volney

Going to Hell.
  —Kevin

I know if I follow what God has put into my heart I will not have to struggle with worldly things. These are material things that make us turn away from God and chase after material happiness, which makes us lose ourselves spiritually.
  —Doaikah

That I continue to depend on the Lord and not fall back to my own understanding.
  —Robert

I understand Satan will be after me when I get out. I have to stay strong, trust God, and stay on the right path.
—Timothy

Return to darkness because of freedom.
—Earl

That people will reject me and the Word of God and not listen to me and keep doing the wrong, sinful things as if it's no big deal.
—Wilfredo

Satan, the world, and the flesh have a lot of temptations.
—Jose

What worries me most about surviving spiritually is the world. A lot of people do good under an umbrella. But when temptation hits you in the face, that's the true test. You need God to carry you day by day in order to survive.
—Rodney

We really like Rodney's image of the umbrella. It's one thing to feel positive and excited when the institutional umbrella keeps temptation and fresh disappointment on the other side of the prison wall. It's another thing when you're outside and the storms come. It's hard to stand tall when the lure of the streets, the pull of old habits you hoped were gone, the unresolved problems with your family, and the disappointments, struggles and frustrations of daily life hit you in the face day after day. Rainy and stormy days lie ahead, and it's best to do some preparation and planning, now, while you're still inside.

Planning and Communicating

For months, Dan dreamed about his Disneyland homecoming. But as he himself pointed out, nothing could have been further from the truth. Even with a safe and stable place waiting for him at home, even with supportive family and friends, and even armed with faith and the best of intentions, Dan's re-entry to the outside world was a bumpy and traumatic one. Looking back on his experience after the fact, what could he have done differently? What could have made his glide path smoother and his landing a more positive one?

One obvious area was his lack of planning. He was so fixated on his release day that he didn't think long and hard about what he would be doing when he got home. He didn't communicate up front with his family about what the expectations would be when he was back. That meant that everything had to be figured out on the spot, further adding to the mess and confusion in his mind. He didn't mentally or spiritually prepare himself for what was surely coming—he was too busy dealing with short-timer's disease. Most of us are notoriously poor planners, of course, but what Dan could really have benefited from was the boring, painstaking work of making practical plans *and* communicating them with his family.

We recently came across a helpful pre-release "communication checklist" that could have saved Dan some grief. Not every question would have applied directly to him (or to you), and there are some guys who have burned all their bridges, but we thought this was something that you might want to hang on to. At the very least, even if you can't find a way to work through this checklist with someone on the outside, it can be helpful preparation for you to work through it in detail.

Communications Checklist

1. Expectations for housing. Where will you live?

2. Expectations for the Big Day (day of release). Who will pick you up? Walk through the day. What will it look like? Who will be present?

3. Expectations for parenting roles. In some cases, custody of the children.

4. Expectations for household responsibilities; who does what (finances, transportation, etc.). Discuss how things have changed and how things are now done at home.

5. Plans for employment or education.

6. Expectations for accountability in the area of time, finances, whereabouts, etc.

7. Expectations for attending church, joining a small group, or meeting with a mentor.

8. Expectations regarding friends. Whom should you associate with or avoid?

9. Substance abuse treatment.

10. Discussing the ways each of you thinks the other has changed.

11. Identifying how the children have changed.

12. Talking about the crime. What needs to be done to heal the harm that was caused?

From Where I Sit: Preparing Yourself for Reentry; Mary Johnson, Prison Fellowship

"Why do I need to prepare myself for reentry? I've been going in and out of jail/prison all my life. I know my mistakes. And besides, I am never coming back here again." Most of the men leaving prison have made this same statement, but somehow they still ended up back in a cell again. The cycle keeps repeating itself. So you have to ask, why? Why do I think this time when I get out it is going to be different? Until you actually look to see the problem, there is no problem.

The Hole in the Sidewalk

I walk down the street. There is a big hole in the sidewalk. I fall in. I am lost. I am helpless. It isn't my fault. It takes forever to find a way out.

I walk down the street. There is a big hole in the sidewalk. I pretend I don't see it. I fall in. I can't believe I'm in the same place, but it isn't my fault. It still takes a long time to get out.

I walk down the street. There is a big hole in the sidewalk. I see it there. I still fall in. It's a habit. My eyes are open. I know where I am. It is my fault. I get out immediately.

I walk down the street. There is a big hole in the sidewalk. I walk around it.

I walk down a different street.

—Author Unknown

Preparation is a gift of time. You choose. You can use your time wisely, or your time will use you. Time will pass slowly, painfully, and purposelessly, if you let it. Or you can use your time to better your circumstances, to increase in knowledge, obtain wisdom and insight, and build physical and emotional strength. Ask yourself, how do you want to return to 'the world'? Do you see yourself doing the same thing you did before, only smarter so you won't get caught? Or do you want to become a man who takes responsibility for his actions, thoughts, emotions, and relationships with others? You choose. There are three basic beliefs about change.

1. People are responsible for their own behavior.

2. People do not begin to change because they see the light, but because they feel the heat.

3. Change is not a one time event, it's a journey.

Preparation is the fun part of any journey. Have you ever planned a trip? You pick a particular destination because it offers you some benefit—something that will be fulfilling in your life. You start by counting the cost before you make the decision to take the journey. The next step is moving your dream into a reality. This is where most people get stuck. As long as it's just a pie-in-the-sky dream, it remains up there with the fluffy clouds just floating by you.

Here is the shift/change needed to establish it. It can be firmed up by creating a road map (plan) with destination points, provisions, stops, rest areas along the way, and planning for possible detours. And with good planning and implementing you can reach your destination and enjoy a rich, full, rewarding life. The life we believe you were destined for by God. "For I know the plans

I have for you," declares the Lord, "plans to prosper you and not to harm you, plans to give you hope and a future" (Jeremiah 29:11).

A group of volunteers from Cook County Jail passed this little acronym along to me after teaching it in their Bible study.

P = Plan: Failure to plan means you plan to fail. How do you get to a destination without a map or clear directions?

L = Learn: Learn something—anything. Use this time to learn about a field of interest that will help with work or is just good fun.

A = Attitude: Attitude is everything; it controls you, your course, and your outcomes. Choose to have a good one.

N = No: Say no to anything and everything that is addictive, destructive, harmful, and cruel.

So whether you are prepared for release or not really depends on you. If you are serious about not returning to prison, get started setting goals and writing out your plan to reach them. Don't wait until you are three weeks out to start this. Tackle first things first. You have just arrived. After you transfer to your permanent facility, you will be able to request to participate in programs, work or education classes. Get started making a list of goals and steps you need to take that will prepare you to reach your God-given potential and destiny.

Common Short-term In-Prison Goals

• Learn a trade or get a marketable skill.

• Participate in education programs. Get your GED or (at some facilities) take college courses.

- Participate in substance abuse treatment classes and mental health courses/counseling.

- Participate in religious services and workshops or programs offered at your facility.

- Modify (abate) your child support order if needed.

- Keep in touch with family members weekly. Don't adopt the attitude that you will set things right when you get out. You can be a good father/husband/son right now if you stay connected. Write.

- Obtain your social security card and birth certificate, and any other documents you will need.

- Develop a resume. Gather data for job applications: Employers, dates, times, contacts, references.

- Practice interviewing for a job. Practice a positive 60-second response to the "felony" question on every application. Memorize that answer; make it short, positive, and powerful. No sob stories.

- Work with your case manager to prepare for release. Clear any aliases.

- Complete in-prison reentry programs: Lifestyle ReDirect, Job Prep, Track, and Re-entry Summits.

- Consider and research finding a positive place to live when released.

- If applicable, obtain documents to apply for government benefits needed prior to release.

- Learn—master a skill; become a peer facilitator within the system, e.g., HIV awareness.

- List debts, and create a plan for re-paying as able, or upon release. Write creditors regarding your incarceration, especially credit card companies. They sometimes reduce or suspend debt.

- Create a list of five supportive and responsible people who can help you upon release.

- Exercise. Keep your physical body in shape. Choose a low-fat, low-sodium diet.

- Establish connections to resources and people that help you grow stronger spiritually, emotionally, mentally, and physically, and that bring hope and encouragement.

- Journal—capture your inspired thoughts, wisdom or lessons you've learned, a vision for your future.

When writing a goal, try applying the S.A.M. method to keep it simple. Ask yourself if the goal is

S = Specific

A = Achievable

M = Measurable

When writing your action steps to attain the goal, ask yourself who, what, where, why, how, and when! These simple questions will help solidify the goal.

If I told you my goal was to be more loving, you might say, "Why, that is such a good thing!" But the truth is there is no way to know if I will ever meet this goal because it is not very specific. So let's say I told you I intended to be more loving to my mother-in-law. That would be more specific. But I did not say how I was going to do this or when, so the goal is not measurable, and we don't know if I can achieve it. So let's say I told you that I intended to be more loving to my mother-in-law by calling her every week and sending her a card or gift on her birthday and on Mother's Day. That would certainly be more measurable, and you could hold me accountable by asking, "Did you call your mother-in-law this week?" Applying S.A.M. makes it a solid goal, not just a good idea.

Working your goals requires diligence and determination along with hard work. But it pays off, and it will fill your days ahead with lots of positive activities. You may find yourself too busy to get in trouble and too busy to get caught up in prison mind games. "The lazy man craves and gets nothing, but the desires of the diligent are fully satisfied" (Proverbs 13:4).

When you are nearing release, write Prison Fellowship for a free copy of Shortimer, Preparing for Release at 44180 Riverside Parkway, Lansdowne, VA 20176.

Surviving Spiritually at the Speed of Life

Planning and preparing are essential. Without it, your chances of a good re-entry into society are slim to none. But even with the best planning and preparing, even when filled with God-given hope and realistic expectations, the transition to surviving spiritually on the outside is a tremendous challenge. Right now you have time—time that you won't have on the outside. Right now you aren't having to make many decisions. In fact, you're not being encouraged to make any decisions. But on the outside, decisions will come at you fast and furiously. Right now your freedoms are severely restricted. On the outside, freedom will present an avalanche of temptations on every street corner. Right now you're dealing with a difficult set of spiritual issues. On the outside you'll be dealing with a whole new set of spiritual issues. Right now, you're dealing with things at normal speed. On the outside, you'll be dealing with things at "game speed." By saying that, we're not trying to scare or intimidate you, or anything like that. But like football coaches who prep their players for what's coming by showing them game film, we'd like to give you a spiritual heads-up on what you may be facing when you get out.

Disorientation. Dan's story did a good job of describing what it feels like in those first days and weeks after release. In a way, it's easier to take your body out of the prison than to take the prison out of your mind. You'll find that, whether you wanted to or not, you grooved in that "prisoner mentality" over the years. That means, in the early days, you'll feel out-of-step with almost everyone—except, perhaps, other ex-convicts (and you may need to stay away from them for legal reasons or for your own good). You'll be experiencing reverse culture shock. Like Dan, you'll probably feel overwhelmed. You may want to go into a shell or go out and medicate yourself. Resist the urge.

> It truly felt like I'd lost whatever mind I had left!
> —Dan

Remember, this experience of being disoriented is normal, and it passes. There's very little you'll be able to do to hurry up the process. It's sort of the equivalent to going outside into bright sunlight after having been in a dark room. Only, instead of just your eyes having to adjust, your thoughts, emotions, and habitual behaviors will need time to adjust to the new environment. The more you realize that this is part of a natural process of readjustment to being outside, the more you can keep from freaking out and losing it in the early weeks. You'll find that you really need to rely on God during this time. Finding reassurance, confidence, and courage to keep things together in prayer will be a major priority. The only problem with that is, just when you really need it, the whole spiritual routine that you've been developing for years behind bars will have been interrupted.

Hitting the spiritual reset button. You can be sure that whatever spiritual growth or depth you manage to develop in prison will be a tremendous asset on the outside. However, you can probably expect that the patterns or habits or schedules that worked well inside will be hard to maintain once you leave prison. The specific times that you set aside for Bible reading, thoughtful reflection, Bible study groups, 12-step groups, and church services will all be gone. Your spiritual buddies will be gone. And all at the same time. You'll need to hit reset. Some guys manage to hit reset and restart their spiritual life on the outside without too much trouble. Other guys seem to have a big disconnect between ending their spiritual life on the inside and starting it fresh on the outside. We asked some ex-inmates on the west side of Chicago about what happened to their relationship with God, their prayer life and their Bible reading in their first six months after prison. They paint a very mixed picture.

> My relationship with God has grown tremendously, and is still growing.

> I prayed more and got closer to God, although I haven't been reading the Bible regularly.

> They all got better.

> It was not as strong as it was in jail.

> I am in God's hands and have been praying every day since 2000.

I gave up and went into a state of depression.

A lot of people pray for me every day, and I pray for myself, and I thank God for that!

I stopped praying and got back into drugs and alcohol.

Hitting reset and setting up new spiritual routines and habits can be a difficult process, especially if you don't get ongoing support or if you find your priorities shifting because of all the new demands on your time and the decisions you have to make.

Decisions, decisions, decisions. Unfortunately, prison does a fantastic job at shielding us from the practice of decision making. Choices as simple as what and when to eat are taken out of our hands. Many of us forget about the sheer number of everyday decisions that have to be made, especially when we re-enter society and have forgotten what that's like.

If it were only a question of deciding on minor things like menu choices, we wouldn't even bother mentioning it. But "big-decision" overload is a whole different thing. Deciding things like whether it's better to live with family or in a half-way house, what kind of jobs to apply for, what old friends to re-connect with or disconnect from, who to trust or not, how and when to resume parenting responsibilities, and dozens of other issues, *simultaneously*, is enough to overwhelm the best of us. We need to find a way to step up and get help at the same time.

Dangerous freedom. Maybe the greatest decision we face is what to do with our new-found freedom. We no longer have people restricting our movement and monitoring where we go. We now have the freedom to walk down those same paths that put us in prison in the first place. That road is clear, and we often have people encouraging us to join them on it. The spiritual question is,

> Am I free enough to say no to this temptation? When I step outside and I hear a car honking, and I see my old crew waving me over to go for a ride with them, does my relationship with God give me the inner strength to tell them that I'm done with all that? Will God give me the courage to stand tall when they're making fun of me and pressuring me, and telling me that I'll be back out in the streets in a week? Will they believe that I've changed? Do I believe that I've changed? Really?

Everything is spiritual. Everything we do reflects on our character, our values, our priorities, and our basic trust in God. For example, looking for a job is a profoundly spiritual exercise, because we need integrity to tell the truth on our job applications. We need patience and perseverance to keep going when we've been rejected fifty times in a row. We need hopefulness and trust to continue to look for legitimate work instead of stealing or selling drugs. We need humility to start a new job as the person who takes orders from everyone else. We need trustworthiness and discipline to show up on time every day in order to hang on to it. And we need gratitude to thank God for the opportunity to work. It's *all* spiritual.

And we could say the same sort of things about getting along with our family, participating in a twelve-step program, taking care of our health, avoiding pornography, helping out at home, taking the initiative to reach out to help others even though we're still in need ourselves, and a thousand other things. Everything is spiritual, because nothing exists outside of God's sphere of influence or concern. Everything is spiritual, because everything is connected, because everything matters to God, and because we matter to God.

Finding a church. With all the churches we have in our neighborhoods, you might think that it would be the easiest and most natural thing in the world for an ex-inmate to find one where he can feel comfortable and productive. *But you'd be wrong.* For all sorts of reasons, bridging back into a church community is tough for lots of us.

It isn't for lack of wanting that to happen. We asked some current inmates about what they'd be looking for in a church when they get out. Here are the kinds of things they told us.

> The truth! A church that has much love for its members who will sacrifice to help the church in moving forward.
> —Jacques

> First the spirit of God's presence—his anointing in the people and the love. No love, no me!
> —Anthony

> One that serves God first and loves men too by good works! One that practices helping people, separated from sin and also has a fivefold ministry: apostles, prophets, teachers, miracles, gifts of healing, etc!
> —JT

> Truly faithful, filled with hope and with as much love as we are expected to have—that would be nice, but in all reality, just one that will greet you and welcome you with open, loving arms is all I would need! Compassion for all others! The light in their eyes!
> —James

> I will be looking for a non-denominational church with a congregation of mixed races and ages. A church that is

Bible-based and not stuck in its own rules and interpretations of Bible doctrine. A church that ministers to all sinners no matter their background.
—Anonymous

Spirit-led people. And people who know how to love others.
—Volney

A church that is built wholly on the truth of the Bible. I want to be encircled with people who do all they can when it comes to helping others.
—Doaikah

One that is fundamentally sound in doctrine, by preaching and of the Bible.
—Robert

A church that will show me the love they have for God and to help me grow in the Word.
—Timothy

Fellowship, guidance, sharing of the word of all, everyone's opinion.
—Earl

The gospel. There's a lot of churches wanting to preach prosperity, gimmicks, social gospel, psycho-babble, but only a few preach the true and living resurrection of Christ, and the free gift of eternity.
—Jose

Bible, love, fellowship, faith, patience, understanding, brothers, sisters, something that will make me feel that that's where I'm supposed to be, that's my home. I want smiles, laughter, being able to sing for the Lord and shout "Amen, Glory to God!" Having the opportunity to speak to everyone around me! The real feeling of love.
—Wilfredo

These are solid, hopeful, understandable, and wonderful things to hope for in a new church community. And these things can, in fact, be found in our neighborhood churches. Unfortunately, the picture they paint looks more like heaven than our local church. And that's because our churches are also full of sinners like ourselves! We can thank God that our churches are full of sinners (there's room for us), but that makes them considerably less appealing than the ideal picture we often conjure up in our head.

Here's what happens all too often: When we show up at a local church and the spiritual temperature is less than we were used to in prison, we can feel let down by the worship experience. When we show up and people welcome us with less than open arms (they're wondering if we're for real, or if we're playing a game), we can feel like they're a bunch of hypocrites. When we show up with our untrusting prison defenses still up, we can behave awkwardly and find it hard to connect with people. When we show up feeling conspicuous and self-conscious because we've been in prison, we can isolate ourselves and end up feeling even more like an outsider than when we walked in.

> I always thought church was just a place to "get high sober" — spiritually and emotionally.
> — Dan

Church is hard because life itself is hard. And yet, with all the things that can (and do) go wrong, finding a church where we can truly worship, contribute, serve, learn, connect, and love and be loved is probably the greatest spiritual gift we can give ourselves. And that's because God made us for community. We're simply never going to thrive spiritually on the outside without being deeply connected to other believers. So whatever else you do, find yourself a church and dig in.

Think About It. Talk About It.

1. If you're still in prison when you're reading this, how much hope do you have for your own good re-entry and for surviving spiritually beyond prison? If you've already been released, how did your first few months of re-entry go?

2. How do you react to Dan's story of going home? Do you think it's fairly typical? Are there any lessons for you in his story?

3. Every inmate who is going home needs both profound hope and realistic expectations. Do you have both things right now, or are you missing one of them?

4. What excites you most about the idea of surviving spiritually beyond prison?

5. How good are you at advance planning? At communicating your plans? If you're not so good at planning or communicating, who could you get to help you to improve? As your release date draws closer, will you use the Communications Checklist?

6. What worries or concerns you most about surviving spiritually after prison?

a) feeling overwhelmed by the pace of life on the outside

b) not setting up a new spiritual support system in time

c) making wise decisions on a consistent basis

d) the streets—not handling my freedom in a God-pleasing way

e) basic life issues—getting a job, relations with my family, etc.

From Where We Sit: Advice From Former Prisoners

- Change what is inside your head. Rethink, relearn, and renew your mind.

- Live right now. Live in prison as you envision you will live when you are back in community—with a positive attitude, responsible behavior, and good healthy habits.

- Set realistic goals and begin taking the necessary steps to achieve them now.

- Be patient with yourself and others. Take one day at a time. Hush the rush!

- Persevere—do not give up! Stay the course and recognize your need to be strengthened.

- Think before you act. One stupid, emotional moment has the ability to set us back.

- No one owes you anything. So don't keep any chips on your shoulder.

- Find out who you are. What is your identity? How are you unique? What are your strengths? Capitalize on them. What are your weaknesses? Know them. This is where you need help from others.

- Maintain an attitude of gratitude; keep a positive focus in every situation.

- Apologize to those you've harmed (whenever possible). Review offenses daily.

- Keep in touch with family members. Rebuild relationships. Be genuine in building bonds of trust.

- Talk to your children. Apologize for not being there. Stay involved. Write or call weekly.

- Treat others with dignity and respect. If you do, you will most likely be treated that way.

- Take time out to read—this book included!

8

BIBLE STUDIES FOR INSIDE AND OUT

We have a vision – and are busy developing resources – for a new kind of Bible study for inmates and returning citizens. We want to explore 101 key Bible passages and then ask engaging questions that connect with our own personal lives. We want to crate a small group environment where we can wrestle with practical spiritual truths that we can start applying, right where we are. No more know-it-all teacher doing all the talking – this is about tapping into the experience, wisdom, and insight of an entire small group. We want to get people thinking and talking to and praying for each other in a healthy, uplifting, supportive way.

We're working hard to launch "Inside Out Network Small Groups" both inside and outside prison. As an inmate, you can find an ION small group and work through the Bibles studies, applying them to your situation while locked up. And then, as a returning citizen, you can continue your spiritual growth by connecting with an ION small group at a church on the outside. It's amazing to see how God's Word applies to us in both places!

As a sampler, we're including the first seven Bible studies. They are the first in a series of 101 studies, patterned on key sections of Jesus' story of the Prodigal Son.

After an initial study of the Prodigal Son story, we go on to six stories of prisoners in the Bible.

Talk to your prison chaplain or let us know if you're interested in getting an ION small group study started in your prison. We'll try our best to get you the study materials you need to make it work well in your setting.

After several years of running ION small groups, we've learned some valuable lessons about what makes a healthy group tick. In fact, we've developed our own small group covenant, similar to AA's "How it Works," which is often read at the start of AA meetings. You might want to consider using it – or use it as inspiration to craft your own.

Here's How It Works for Us

We can't speak for everyone, but here's what we've come to believe: We're here because we tried doing life on our own, apart from God and his church, and it didn't work. We're here because we seriously desire change, and we admit that we need God's help and the help of others. We're here because we need hope that won't fail.

We will discover and live in that hope by meeting for Bible study, honest conversation, and mutual accountability so that – together – we can live changed and restored lives. As we grow, we will seek to meet the spiritual needs of those out there still lost and wondering if hope is real, by inviting them to the new life we've found in Jesus Christ.

Here's how we carry ourselves when we're together:

- Confidentiality – This is a special, intimate group where we are privileged to be very honest and vulnerable with one another. Anything that is said in our meetings is never repeated outside the meetings without permission.

- Respect – We listen to each other and value everyone's right to their opinions as we value our own. All questions are encouraged and respected. Everyone's participation is encouraged, but no one is given permission to dominate the conversation.

- Accountability – We agree to let members of the group hold us accountable to commitments we make, in whatever gentle and loving ways we decide upon. At the same time, giving unsolicited advice is not permitted.

- Relationships – Life change doesn't happen in isolation. We will do our best to bond, provide mutual support and encouragement, grow as disciples of Jesus, and learn to lead.

- Community – By participating in this group we are being given something that others don't have: a place where we belong and are accepted as we really are. We won't keep this to ourselves, but will welcome newcomers and reach out to others in need of help and hope.

Alive Again: Prodigal Son, Prodigal Love

LISTEN

Bitter experience teaches one big truth: we're great at screwing up our lives. An even bigger truth comes straight from Jesus: God's love for screw-ups like us goes beyond anything we could have guessed or imagined. This truth is unforgettably captured in Jesus' parable of the Prodigal. Jesus often taught in parables – short, deceptively simple stories "with intent." Jesus intention is that we might see ourselves, others and the world around us, and God himself in a new and true light – and then respond with a transformed life.

This story has layer after layer of meaning, and it rewards those who come back to it again and again. In many ways, it captures the great drama of our salvation: selfishness and imposed isolation, rupturing of relationships, desperation, bargaining, surprising and amazing grace, unbridled celebration, lingering resentment, unfinished business, the journey from wasted life to alive again.

The story meets us where we are. It comes as comforting good news when we find ourselves falling and hitting bottom. It comes as challenging good news when we find ourselves falling into resentment and judgmentalism. And it comes as inspiring good news when we find ourselves running to help other screw-ups like ourselves encounter the depths of our heavenly Father's love.

The word "prodigal" has often been applied to this story that Jesus told. Prodigal means extravagant, lavish, excessive, even to the point of being wasteful – and it's a good description of the younger son's wasteful life-style. But the word also beautifully describes the father's enduring love for his son – lavish, extravagant, knowing no bounds. The son's prodigal desires led to his ruin. But the father's prodigal love led to his restoration and new life.

READ

11 Jesus said: "There was a man who had two sons. 12 The younger one said to his father, 'Father, give me my share of the estate.' So he divided his property between them. 13 Not long after that, the younger son got together all he had, set off for a distant country and there squandered his wealth in wild living. 14 After he had spent everything, there was a severe famine in that whole country, and he began to be in need. 15 So he went and hired himself out to a citizen of that country, who sent him to his fields to feed pigs. 16 He longed to fill his stomach with the pods that the pigs were eating, but no one gave him anything. 17 When he came to his senses, he said, 'How many of my father's hired servants have food to spare, and here I am starving to death! 18 I will set out and go back to my father and say to him: Father, I have sinned against heaven and against you. 19 I am no longer worthy to be called your son; make me like one of your hired servants.' 20 So he got up and went to his father. But while he was still a long way off, his father saw him and was filled with compassion for him; he ran to his son, threw his arms around him and kissed him.

21 The son said to him, 'Father, I have sinned against heaven and against you. I am no longer worthy to be called your son.' 22 But the father said to his servants, 'Quick! Bring the best robe and put it on him. Put a ring on his finger and sandals on

his feet. 23 Bring the fattened calf and kill it. Let's have a feast and celebrate. 24 For this son of mine was dead and is alive again; he was lost and is found.' So they began to celebrate. 25 Meanwhile, the older son was in the field. When he came near the house, he heard music and dancing. 26 So he called one of the servants and asked him what was going on. 27 'Your brother has come,' he replied, 'and your father has killed the fattened calf because he has him back safe and sound.' 28 The older brother became angry and refused to go in. So his father went out and pleaded with him. 29 But he answered his father, 'Look! All these years I've been slaving for you and never disobeyed your orders. Yet you never gave me even a young goat so I could celebrate with my friends. 30 But when this son of yours who has squandered your property with prostitutes comes home, you kill the fattened calf for him!' 31 'My son,' the father said, 'you are always with me, and everything I have is yours. 32 But we had to celebrate and be glad, because this brother of yours was dead and is alive again; he was lost and is found.'
~Luke 15:11-32

DISCUSS

We offer suggestions for some possible answers, but don't feel confined by them.

1. Why do you think the younger son left home?

    a. It was boring and confining.
    b. He wanted to walk on the wild side.
    c. To be free of his family's values.
    d. He was self-centered.
    e. He was self-destructive.

2. What made the younger son return? What made him come to his senses?

a. Desperation, pure and simple.

b. He saw through the emptiness of the life he had chosen.

c. He finally realized how good it was back home.

d. He finally hit bottom. Before that happened, he was never going to turn around.

e. He thought he could bargain with the old man.

3. If you had been the father in this story, what would you have been thinking and feeling?

a. I would have been furious that my son asked me for his inheritance – he couldn't wait for me to die!

b. I would have been worried sick while my son was gone.

c. I would have felt sad that my son was trying to bargain with me when he returned.

d. I would have made him learn a lesson by making him stay in the dog house for a while.

e. I would have felt frustrated and sad that my older son wouldn't come in to celebrate.

f. I would have felt joy – my son is alive again!

4. If you had been the older son in this story, what would you have been thinking and feeling?

a. I hate the little punk for shaming our family.

b. I'm furious with my father for enabling my little brother and then celebrating his return.

c. I feel taken for granted.

d. I feel torn: glad my brother survived, but unhappy that he's back.

e. Resentful: It's going to take a long time for me to let this go.

f. My father has a point. I need to shift my emotions from anger to joy.

5. Who do you most identify with in this story? In what ways do your own experiences mirror the characters in the story?

6. What qualities do you admire most in the father?

   a. His willingness to let the younger son have his way – he wasn't controlling.
   b. His patience as he waited for his son's return.
   c. The depth of his merciful love.
   d. His ability to love both of his sons.
   e. He knows how to party!

7. What stage(s) of the prodigal son's journey most match where you are right now?

   a. I'm still in that "distant country" pursuing wild living – far from God and family.
   b. I've had enough time in the pig slop. I'm finally coming to my senses.
   c. I'm still trying to figure out how to bargain with my heavenly Father.
   d. I'm feeling the loving embrace of my heavenly Father.
   e. I'm currently dealing with some enduring resentment from my family.
   f. It's been a long and winding road, but I'm finally alive again!

8. What's the hardest part of Jesus' parable for you to wrap your mind around?

   a. I wonder why the prodigal son ever left home since he had it so good.
   b. I wonder why the older son stayed home since he felt taken for granted.
   c. I wonder why the father didn't just say no to the younger son in the beginning.

d. I wonder how the two brothers are going to reconcile. Who and what needs to change?

e. I'm awestruck, because Jesus was teaching us that our heavenly Father loves each one of us prodigal sons and daughters like the father in this parable.

PRAY

Pray for each other, for those still inside, and for those outside.

Prisoners in the Bible: I Was in Prison

LISTEN

Life is a wonderful gift from God. But life is also hard. Often it's a struggle just to make it through the day. Sometimes we're the ones who are in need and suffer, and sometimes it's the people around us. And all of this neediness and suffering raises two important questions: How much does God care about people in need? And how much do we?

In this passage, Jesus talks about the great "sorting-out" process that he'll be in charge of at the end of time. In the process, he gives us some crucial insights into how he answers those questions.

1. Jesus deeply cares about everyone in need, and he expects those who say that they know and follow him to care about them too.

2. Jesus specifically cares about prisoners, and he expects those who say that they know and follow him to actively care for them too.

3. Jesus not only cares about prisoners, he personally identifies with them. He is not only for them or with them. It goes deeper: He *is* them.

4. What we think about Jesus is measured by how we treat those in need.

As we read and discuss Jesus' teaching, ask yourself if God has a word of comfort, encouragement, or warning for you today.

READ

31 Jesus said, "When the Son of Man comes in his glory, and all the angels with him, he will sit on his glorious throne. 32 All the nations will be gathered before him, and he will separate the people one from another as a shepherd separates the sheep from the goats. 33 He will put the sheep on his right and the goats on his left.

34 "Then the King will say to those on his right, 'Come, you who are blessed by my Father; take your inheritance, the kingdom prepared for you since the creation of the world. 35 For I was hungry and you gave me something to eat, I was thirsty and you gave me something to drink, I was a stranger and you invited me in, 36 I needed clothes and you clothed me, I was sick and you looked after me, I was in prison and you came to visit me.'

37 "Then the righteous will answer him, 'Lord, when did we see you hungry and feed you, or thirsty and give you something to drink? 38 When did we see you a stranger and invite you in, or needing clothes and clothe you? 39 When did we see you sick or in prison and go to visit you?'

40 "The King will reply, 'Truly I tell you, whatever you did for one of the least of these brothers and sisters of mine, you did for me.'

41 "Then he will say to those on his left, 'Depart from me, you who are cursed, into the eternal fire prepared for the devil and his angels. 42 For I was hungry and you gave me nothing to eat, I was thirsty and you gave me nothing to drink, 43 I was a stranger and you did not invite me in, I needed clothes and you did not clothe me, I was sick and in prison and you did not look after me.'

44 "They also will answer, 'Lord, when did we see you hungry or thirsty or a stranger or needing clothes or sick or in prison, and did not help you?' 45 He will reply, 'Truly I tell you, whatever you did not do for one of the least of these, you did not do for me.' 46 Then they will go away to eternal punishment, but the righteous to eternal life."—Matthew 25:31-46

DISCUSS

We offer suggestions for some possible answers, but don't feel confined by them.

1. During your own imprisonment, did you get visits?

   a. A lot.
   b. Some, but it showed me who my real friends were.
   c. Never.
   d. No, I burned my bridges.
   e. Yes, from volunteers.

2. How did visits make you feel?

   a. Like I hadn't been forgotten.
   b. Like a nervous wreck.
   c. Mixed. They were great during the visit, but I felt more depressed afterward.
   d. Awkward and angry. They were too short and controlled.
   e. They were a lifeline for me.

3. How does the idea of Jesus himself, needy and in prison, identifying with those who are locked up, make you feel?

   a. Confused. Why would he do that?

b. Reassured and comforted that I'm not alone, even in the worst of times.

c. Encouraged that he knows what I've gone through.

d. Amazed that he cares that much.

4. Over the years, how well have taken care of those in need? Have you been more a "goat" or more a "sheep"?

a. Sadly, I've been a total goat—too busy with my own needs.

b. More goat than sheep—I realize now how many missed opportunities there were to care for others.

c. Half-sheep, half-goat—but I was always pretty selective with who I helped.

d. More sheep than goat—I've always been pretty tuned-in to those who are in need.

5. How well do you respond to the needs of the following people in need? Are you drawn to serve some more than others? Why or why not?

a. those who are hungry or in need of shelter

b. strangers

c. those who are sick

d. prisoners

6. How well do you think most churches do when it comes to visiting those in prison? What's been your own experience?

a. Unfortunately, out of sight, out of mind.

b. They're well-intentioned, but confused about how to help.

c. They're afraid and want to keep their distance.

d. They're judgmental and don't want us in their life.

e. They're ashamed to show their face at the prison door.

f. They're doing the best they can.

7. What do you think of being called one of "the least of these brothers and sisters of mine" by Jesus?

a. Offended—I'm not "least."

b. Elated—Jesus calls me his brother.

c. I'm okay with it. It captures both the difficulty and the dignity of our situation.

8. As you stop to reflect on your own experience and that of others, what could be done to make prison visits better and more frequent?

9. What's your big takeaway from this teaching by Jesus?

a. Comfort—Jesus identifies with me.

b. Encouragement—the small things I do for those in need really matter to God.

c. Warning—this is a wake-up call for me. I need to wake up to the need around me and start helping others.

PRAY

Pray for each other, for those still inside, and for those outside.

Prisoners in the Bible: Cain and Abel

LISTEN

Crime and punishment. Resentment and temptation. Violence and murder. We're surrounded by all of this, but none of it is new. In fact, it's as old as the first human family. It's easy to see what happens when things go terribly wrong in our families and in our cities. What's harder to see is why. Why are people acting the way they do? What's going on under the surface?

These are the kinds of questions God's Word starts to explore right from the beginning of the Bible. Just after describing God's creation of human beings and our Fall into brokenness and sin, we get the story of two brothers, Cain and Abel. It's partly a story of sibling rivalry escalating into violence, but it's so much more. Above all, it's an exploration of God's relationship to us and his response to our violent tendencies.

The story starts with an act of worship. Cain and Abel both bring an offering to God—each one offers up something of their own to God. But something goes wrong right off the bat. It turns out that there's something defective and unacceptable with Cain's offering. There's something mysterious and unspoken going on here. Abel seems to have given sacrificially to God, offering up the "choice cuts" to God. Cain, on the other hand, seems to have given "something, but nothing special." Something is in motion, and it won't end until one of them is dead and the other is living a cursed, though protected existence under God's care.

As we read and discuss this story of Cain and Abel, ask yourself what we can learn from God's Word about human nature and God's character.

READ

1 Adam made love to his wife Eve, and she became pregnant and gave birth to Cain. She said, "With the help of the LORD I have brought forth a man." 2 Later she gave birth to his brother Abel.

Now Abel kept flocks, and Cain worked the soil. 3 In the course of time Cain brought some of the fruits of the soil as an offering to the LORD. 4 And Abel also brought an offering—fat portions from some of the firstborn of his flock. The LORD looked with favor on Abel and his offering, 5 but on Cain and his offering he did not look with favor. So Cain was very angry, and his face was downcast.

6 Then the LORD said to Cain, "Why are you angry? Why is your face downcast? 7 If you do what is right, will you not be accepted? But if you do not do what is right, sin is crouching at your door; it desires to have you, but you must rule over it."

8 Now Cain said to his brother Abel, "Let's go out to the field." While they were in the field, Cain attacked his brother Abel and killed him.

9 Then the LORD said to Cain, "Where is your brother Abel?"

"I don't know," he replied. "Am I my brother's keeper?"

10 The LORD said, "What have you done? Listen! Your brother's blood cries out to me from the ground. 11 Now you are under a curse and driven from the ground, which opened its mouth to receive your brother's blood from your hand. 12 When you work the ground, it will no longer yield its crops for you. You will be a restless wanderer on the earth."

13 Cain said to the LORD, "My punishment is more than I can bear. 14 Today you are driving me from the land, and I will be hidden from your presence; I will be a restless wanderer on the earth, and whoever finds me will kill me."

15 But the LORD said to him, "Not so; anyone who kills Cain will suffer vengeance seven times over." Then the LORD put a mark on Cain so that no one who found him would kill him. 16 So Cain went out from the LORD's presence and lived in the land of Nod, east of Eden.—Genesis 4:1-16

DISCUSS

We offer suggestions for some possible answers, but don't feel confined by them.

1. What made Cain and Abel so different?

a. Cain was just a "bad seed."
b. Initially, not very much. But Cain let sin take him down a terrible road.
c. Younger brothers can be jerks sometimes.
d. Abel's generous gift reveals that he was more interested in his relationship with God than Cain was.

2. Why was Cain angry and who was he angry at?

a. He was angry at God for being displeased with his offering.
b. He was angry at God for looking with favor on his brother.
c. He was angry at Abel for showing him up.
d. He was angry at himself and ashamed for not being "acceptable."

3. Have you ever felt angry and downcast because you felt that God (or

other people) didn't accept you or what you had to offer? If so, how did you handle it?

a. I lashed out at others.

b. I lashed out at myself and beat myself up about it.

c. I shut down inside.

d. I isolated myself from others.

e. I self-medicated.

4. God tried to encourage Cain to do the acceptable thing and warned him about sin crouching at his door like a wild beast. Cain gave in to the beast. How are you doing with the beast these days?

a. Honestly, I welcome the beast in and feed it all too often.

b. I'm keeping the door locked tight.

c. I'm getting help and driving it farther away.

d. It's an ongoing struggle for me.

5. What do you make of Cain's reaction when he was confronted by God after killing Abel?

a. He was evasive and untruthful.

b. He was callous when he said, "Am I my brother's keeper?"

c. He was scared of being punished.

d. He was feeling sorry for himself, like he was the victim, instead of his dead brother.

e. He never seems to have truly repented. He made it all about himself.

6. Cain lived under a curse and was a "restless wanderer" as a result of his behavior. How about you?

a. That pretty much describes my experience. I've just gotten used to it.

b. I used to be that way when I was younger, but I'm finding my way home.

c. Like Cain, I sometimes feel like it's more than I can bear.

d. I'm happy to say that I've been able to keep connected with others.

7. Like the prodigal son, Cain finds himself in a "distant country," the land of Nod, east of Eden. Though the Bible doesn't describe his life there, how do you think it went?

a. Still cursed.

b. Still restless, because he was a "marked man."

c. Difficult, but manageable, because God had marked him to protect him.

d. I'd like to think that he later repented and reestablished his relationship with God.

8. What does this story tell you about the character of the Lord?

a. God always tells the truth, no matter how painful.

b. God is out to get us.

c. God can't be fooled.

d. God cares about the innocent.

e. God is unfair and unpredictable.

f. God is firm, but merciful, with the guilty.

PRAY

Pray for each other, for those still inside, and for those outside.

Prisoners in the Bible: Joseph in Prison

LISTEN

The story of Joseph is one of the longest, most fascinating, and most meaningful stories in the Bible. This is just one of many episodes. Here's the story so far: Joseph has been rejected and betrayed by his brothers, and sold into slavery. He is living in Egypt, far from home. You might think that things couldn't get any worse, but you'd be wrong. They do. Much worse.

As we read and discuss this episode from the life of Joseph and watch him in action, let's explore what God's Word might be teaching us about resisting temptation, being a survivor, making the most of our situation, and living with integrity in the face of ongoing injustice.

READ

Now Joseph had been taken down to Egypt. Potiphar, an Egyptian who was one of Pharaoh's officials, the captain of the guard, bought him from the Ishmaelites who had taken him there. 2 The Lord was with Joseph so that he prospered, and he lived in the house of his Egyptian master. 3 When his master saw that the Lord was with him and that the Lord gave him success in everything he did, 4 Joseph found favor in his eyes and became his attendant. Potiphar put him in charge of his household, and he entrusted to his care everything he owned. 5 From the time he put him in charge of his household and of all that he owned, the

Lord blessed the household of the Egyptian because of Joseph. The blessing of the Lord was on everything Potiphar had, both in the house and in the field. 6 So Potiphar left everything he had in Joseph's care; with Joseph in charge, he did not concern himself with anything except the food he ate.

Now Joseph was well–built and handsome, 7 and after a while his master's wife took notice of Joseph and said, "Come to bed with me!"

8 But he refused. "With me in charge," he told her, "my master does not concern himself with anything in the house; everything he owns he has entrusted to my care. 9 No one is greater in this house than I am. My master has withheld nothing from me except you, because you are his wife. How then could I do such a wicked thing and sin against God?" 10 And though she spoke to Joseph day after day, he refused to go to bed with her or even be with her.

11 One day he went into the house to attend to his duties, and none of the household servants was inside. 12 She caught him by his cloak and said, "Come to bed with me!" But he left his cloak in her hand and ran out of the house. 13 When she saw that he had left his cloak in her hand and had run out of the house, 14 she called her household servants. "Look," she said to them, "this Hebrew has been brought to us to make sport of us! He came in here to sleep with me, but I screamed. 15 When he heard me scream for help, he left his cloak beside me and ran out of the house." 16 She kept his cloak beside her until his master came home. 17 When she told him this story: "That Hebrew slave you brought us came to me to make sport of me. 18 But as soon as I screamed for help, he left his cloak beside me and ran out of the house."

19 When his master heard the story his wife told him, saying, "This is how your slave treated me," he burned with anger. 20 Joseph's master took him and put him in prison, the place where the king's prisoners were confined. But while Joseph was there in the prison, 21 the Lord was with him; he showed him kindness and granted him favor in the eyes of the prison warden. 22 So the warden put Joseph in charge of all those held in the prison, and he was made responsible for all that was done there. 23 The warden paid no attention to anything under Joseph's care, because the Lord was with Joseph and gave him success in whatever he did.—Genesis 39:1-23

DISCUSS

We offer suggestions for some possible answers, but don't feel confined by them.

1. How do you think Joseph felt when he was thrown into prison?

a. Scared, like everyone else.

b. Like a victim, twice over.

c. Like a chump for doing the right thing. No good deed goes unpunished!

d. Cynical—no one can be trusted.

e. Angry at everyone.

f. Angry at God.

g. Like always, determined to make the best of a bad situation.

h. Confident that God would somehow help him out of yet another bad situation.

2. How did you feel when you went to prison?

   a. Betrayed by my friends.

   b. Betrayed by the system.

   c. Betrayed by God.

   d. Disappointed in myself.

   e. Anxious for my future.

   f. Depressed by my situation.

3. Joseph was literally living in a "distant country" as an enslaved foreigner, a stranger in a strange land. His family would eventually follow him there and live, at least initially, as "resident aliens" and economic refugees. Given America's historical record with both slavery and immigration, what parallels do you see, if any?

4. The story says that even though he was unjustly locked up and forgotten on an indeterminate sentence, "while Joseph was there in the prison, the LORD was with him; he showed him kindness and granted him favor in the eyes of the warden." How does that description compare with your own experience of being locked up? How has the Lord been with you in prison?

5. Joseph had been victimized and was innocent of the charges brought against him, and yet he found himself in prison. What's your best guess about how many innocent people end up in prison today? What reasons do you have for saying that?

PRAY

Pray for each other, for those still inside, and for those outside.

Prisoners in the Bible: Peter in Prison

LISTEN

When it comes to issues facing inmates and ex-offenders, this story about Peter hits the mother lode: cruel political games, people used as pawns, fervent prayer, God's power showing up in the darkest places, release for the captives, the important place of the church, the confusion of reentry. A couple of background notes to the story:

- The story takes place after the death and resurrection of Jesus. A new community of his followers has sprung up in the city of Jerusalem. A popular Jesus movement is surfacing, but this movement is seen as a dangerous sect by some in the Jewish community.

- The Jewish puppet-king, Herod, is a cruel political creature and is willing to persecute the Christians if it wins him political power.

- Peter is one of Jesus' key followers and the acknowledged leader of the Jerusalem church.

- Ancient prisons were very different from modern facilities. Most of them were little more than temporary holding facilities for a day or two. The facility that Peter found himself in would probably have been maximum security for its day. Once a legal hearing was held, one of four outcomes normally happened: (1) charges were dismissed, (2) a fine was paid, (3) corporal punishment was immediately administered, or (4) capital punishment was immediately administered. There were some notable exceptions, but by and large, there was no long-term prison sentence behind bars.

As we read and discuss what happens to Peter as he undergoes arrest, detention, release, and reentry, let's see what God's Word might be saying to us about those very things.

READ

1 It was about this time that King Herod arrested some who belonged to the church, intending to persecute them. 2 He had James, the brother of John, put to death with the sword. 3 When he saw that this met with approval among the Jews, he proceeded to seize Peter also. This happened during the Festival of Unleavened Bread. 4 After arresting him, he put him in prison, handing him over to be guarded by four squads of four soldiers each. Herod intended to bring him out for public trial after the Passover.

5 So Peter was kept in prison, but the church was earnestly praying to God for him.

6 The night before Herod was to bring him to trial, Peter was sleeping between two soldiers, bound with two chains, and sentries stood guard at the entrance. 7 Suddenly an angel of the Lord appeared and a light shone in the cell. He struck Peter on the side and woke him up. "Quick, get up!" he said, and the chains fell off Peter's wrists. 8 Then the angel said to him, "Put on your clothes and sandals." And Peter did so. "Wrap your cloak around you and follow me," the angel told him. 9 Peter followed him out of the prison, but he had no idea that what the angel was doing was really happening; he thought he was seeing a vision. 10 They passed the first and second guards and came to the iron gate leading to the city. It opened for them by itself, and they went through it. When they had walked the length of

one street, suddenly the angel left him. 11 Then Peter came to himself and said, "Now I know without a doubt that the Lord has sent his angel and rescued me from Herod's clutches and from everything the Jewish people were hoping would happen." 12 When this had dawned on him, he went to the house of Mary the mother of John, also called Mark, where many people had gathered and were praying. 13 Peter knocked at the outer entrance, and a servant named Rhoda came to answer the door. 14 When she recognized Peter's voice, she was so overjoyed she ran back without opening it and exclaimed, "Peter is at the door!" 15 "You're out of your mind," they told her. When she kept insisting that it was so, they said, "It must be his angel."

16 But Peter kept on knocking, and when they opened the door and saw him, they were astonished. 17 Peter motioned with his hand for them to be quiet and described how the Lord had brought him out of prison. "Tell James and the other brothers and sisters about this," he said, and then he left for another place. 18 In the morning, there was no small commotion among the soldiers as to what had become of Peter. 19 After Herod had a thorough search made for him and did not find him, he cross-examined the guards and ordered that they be executed. Then Herod went from Judea to Caesarea and stayed there.—Acts 12:1-19

DISCUSS

We offer suggestions for some possible answers, but don't feel confined by them.

1. What's your first reaction to this story?

   a. Sounds like a fairy tale.

   b. Sounds like every prisoner's fantasy.

   c. Where's my angel?

   d. There's power in prayer.

   e. There's more power in prayer than we realize.

   f. Sounds like heads are going to roll at the DOC!

   g. God can make a way when there seems to be no way out.

2. What were Herod's motivations at the beginning and end of this story?

   a. Purely political—only interested in what's in it for him.

   b. Flexing his muscles to show everyone who was boss.

   c. He was afraid of the Christian movement—every tyrant is secretly afraid.

   d. Master of the "blame game"—first blame the Christians, then blame the guards.

3. If a "messenger of the Lord" came to you (inside of prison, or out) and said, "Quick, get up! I'll show you the way to real freedom," how would you react?

   a. I'd suspect that it was a con game of some kind.

   b. I'd suspect, like Peter, that I was dreaming.

   c. Are you kidding? I'd jump at the chance.

   d. I'd probably slow everything down and insist on knowing every single step going forward.

   e. My chains didn't fall off miraculously, but God did a kind of miracle getting me home in one piece, in my right mind, and on the way to freedom.

4. What do you think was going on with the church prayer meeting?

a. Their prayer was answered.

b. They were praying, but they never expected it to be answered in such a stunning way.

c. They prayed, but they didn't truly expect the prayer to be answered.

d. God would have rescued Peter whether they prayed or not.

e. I would give anything to have people pray for me like that.

5. Peter had to keep knocking at the door to be let in by his own people, because his knocking was met (at first) by confusion, excitement, disbelief, and astonishment. How does that compare with the reception you got (or are expecting to get) from friends and family?

a. My family doesn't want me back.

b. I'm still knocking at the door.

c. I actually think I need to keep my distance from them for a while.

d. Peter didn't have to start his life over. I do.

PRAY

Pray for each other, for those still inside, and for those outside.

Prisoners in the Bible:
Paul and Silas in Prison

LISTEN

The Bible has more prison scenes than you might expect. Jesus himself and many of his followers found themselves in the hands of the local authorities, whether they were actually guilty or not. Paul, one of the most famous leaders in the early church, found himself locked up again and again. This is a story of one of those many lockups.

First, a couple of background notes:

- Even though he was a prominent leader of a persecuted group, Paul had something that set him apart from many others—his Roman citizenship. It wasn't by any means a get-out-of-jail-free card, but it did give him a recognized legal status that ensured he wouldn't be treated with the same callous disregard that most people faced. In a way, it meant that he "had connections" and enjoyed a certain entitlement.

- This story showcases an important dimension of prison life—the officers who work there. It shows what God's power and grace can do even in the troubled relationship between guards and prisoners.

- Ancient prisons were very different from modern facilities. Most of them were little more than temporary holding facilities for a day or two. Once a legal hearing was held, one of four outcomes normally happened: (1) charges were dismissed, (2) a fine was paid, (3) corporal punishment was immediately administered, or (4) capital punishment was immediately administered. There were some notable exceptions, but, by and large, there was no long-term prison sentence behind bars.

As we read and discuss this remarkable episode, pay close attention to Paul's behavior, character, and priorities in the face of injustice. What inspiration or insight can we draw from God's Word in the midst of our trials?

READ

16 Once when we were going to the place of prayer, we were met by a female slave who had a spirit by which she predicted the future. She earned a great deal of money for her owners by fortune–telling. 17 She followed Paul and the rest of us, shouting, "These men are servants of the Most High God, who are telling you the way to be saved." 18 She kept this up for many days. Finally Paul became so annoyed that he turned around and said to the spirit, "In the name of Jesus Christ I command you to come out of her!" At that moment the spirit left her.

19 When her owners realized that their hope of making money was gone, they seized Paul and Silas and dragged them into the marketplace to face the authorities. 20 They brought them before the magistrates and said, "These men are Jews, and are throwing our city into an uproar 21 by advocating customs unlawful for us Romans to accept or practice." 22 The crowd joined in the attack against Paul and Silas, and the magistrates ordered them to be stripped and beaten with rods. 23 After they had been severely flogged, they were thrown into prison, and the jailer was commanded to guard them carefully. 24 When he received these orders, he put them in the inner cell and fastened their feet in the stocks.

25 About midnight Paul and Silas were praying and singing hymns to God, and the other prisoners were listening to them. 26 Suddenly there was such a violent earthquake that the foundations of the prison were shaken. At once all the prison doors flew open, and everyone's chains came loose. 27 The jailer woke up, and when he saw the prison doors open, he drew his sword and was about to kill himself because he thought the prisoners had escaped. 28 But Paul shouted, "Don't harm yourself! We are all here!" 29 The jailer called for lights, rushed in and fell trembling before Paul and Silas. 30 He then brought them out and asked, "Sirs, what must I do to be saved?"

31 They replied, "Believe in the Lord Jesus, and you will be saved—you and your household." 32 Then they spoke the word of the Lord to him and to all the others in his house. 33 At that hour of the night the jailer took them and washed their wounds; then immediately he and all his household were baptized. 34 The jailer brought them into his house and set a meal before them; he was filled with joy because he had come to believe in God—he and his whole household. 35 When it was daylight, the magistrates sent their officers to the jailer with the order: "Release those men." 36 The jailer told Paul, "The magistrates have ordered that you and Silas be released. Now you can leave. Go in peace."

37 But Paul said to the officers: "They beat us publicly without a trial, even though we are Roman citizens, and threw us into prison. And now do they want to get rid of us quietly? No! Let them come themselves and escort us out." 38 The officers reported this to the magistrates, and when they heard that Paul and Silas were Roman citizens, they were alarmed. 39 They came to appease them and escorted them from the prison, requesting them

to leave the city. 40 After Paul and Silas came out of the prison, they went to Lydia's house, where they met with the believers and encouraged them. Then they left.—Acts 16:16-40

DISCUSS

We offer suggestions for some possible answers, but don't feel confined by them.

1. After all they'd been through, at "about midnight" Paul and Silas are praying out loud and singing hymns to God. What does that make you think?

   a. I've known inmates like that.
   b. I've done something like that.
   c. Get to sleep already!
   d. It's great to have a faithful cellmate so you can encourage each other.
   e. Preach it, brother!
   f. How can anyone have faith like that?
   g. I want faith like that!

2. The story says that the other prisoners were listening to Paul and Silas. Prisoners tend to watch each other very carefully. Do you have any personal examples of inmates who, like Paul and Silas, were positive influences on those around them? Share what these people did and the impact it had on you.

3. The earthquake damage and the loss of security put the jailer in a no-win situation with his superiors. What do you think about the jailer in this story?

   a. Sorry, but I despise those guys.
   b. He's just making a buck and feeding his family.

c. The "correctional" system messes with us all.

d. His reaction to the earthquake shows that he's just as lost as anyone else.

4. Paul had compassion on his jailer, stayed put, shared the gospel with him, baptized him and his family, shared a meal with him, and filled him with joy. Could you imagine doing that with any correctional officers you've known? Why or why not? What would that say about the power of God?

5. Paul and Silas refused to take their unjust and undeserved punishment quietly. They demanded a hearing with the authorities. What impression do you think they made on the jailers? What's your impression of them?

a. They were gutsy.

b. They were foolish.

c. They had great faith.

d. They had great integrity.

PRAY

Pray for each other, for those still inside, and for those outside.

Prisoners in the Bible: Freedom for the Captives

LISTEN

The experience of finding ourselves living like a wayward, prodigal son in a "distant country"—cut off, isolated, far from home—is nothing new to God's people. It happens to many of us on a personal level and it can happen on a national level, too.

God's beloved people, Israel, literally found themselves in a distant country. Their callous disregard and rejection of God eventually led to massive defeat at the hands of their enemies and exile to Babylon—living as captives and strangers in a strange land for generations. But this exile was not forever. God promised deliverance. The prophet Isaiah saw the days of God's Servant (Jesus identified himself with Isaiah's servant figure) announcing the news of the Great Reversal, the Great Restoration, the Lord's favor. This passage says something powerful about who God is and what his heart is like.

As we read and discuss this promise of freedom for the captive people of Israel, ask yourself what we can learn from God's Word about trusting in God's promises of restoration for our own lives.

READ

1 The Spirit of the Sovereign LORD is on me,
because the LORD has anointed me
to proclaim good news to the poor.

He has sent me to bind up the brokenhearted,
to proclaim freedom for the captives
and release from darkness for the prisoners,
2 to proclaim the year of the LORD's favor
and the day of vengeance of our God,
to comfort all who mourn,
3 and provide for those who grieve in Zion—
to bestow on them a crown of beauty
instead of ashes,
the oil of joy
instead of mourning,
and a garment of praise
instead of a spirit of despair.
They will be called oaks of righteousness,
a planting of the LORD
for the display of his splendor.

4 They will rebuild the ancient ruins
and restore the places long devastated;
they will renew the ruined cities
that have been devastated for generations.
5 Strangers will shepherd your flocks;
foreigners will work your fields and vineyards.
6 And you will be called priests of the LORD,
you will be named ministers of our God.
You will feed on the wealth of nations,
and in their riches you will boast.

7 Instead of your shame
you will receive a double portion,
and instead of disgrace
you will rejoice in your inheritance.

And so you will inherit a double portion in your land,
and everlasting joy will be yours.

8 "For I, the LORD, love justice;
I hate robbery and wrongdoing.
In my faithfulness I will reward my people
and make an everlasting covenant with them.
9 Their descendants will be known among the nations
and their offspring among the peoples.
All who see them will acknowledge
that they are a people the LORD has blessed."—Isaiah 61:1-9

DISCUSS

We offer suggestions for some possible answers, but don't feel confined
by them.

1. What must this news have felt like to the Jewish captives in exile
   when they heard this promise of deliverance from God?

2. Does this feel like the "year of the LORD's favor" for you? Why or
   why not?

3. When God's great reversal comes, and when freedom and release
   come for the captives, what's the appropriate response for them to
   have?

   a. Payback—Stick it to those who stuck it to you.
   b. Relief—The nightmare is over.
   c. Gratitude—God is faithful and kept his promise.
   d. Resentment—What took so long?
   e. Joy—We've been blessed!
   f. Confusion—Okay, what next?

g. Apathy—I'm too messed up to care at this stage.

h. Fatalism—It's just a big revolving door; I'll be back in prison again soon.

4. Who is God calling and anointing you to go preach the good news to? To comfort? To bring gladness and praise instead of mourning and despair?

5. What images from Isaiah appeal to you most? Why?

a. Freedom for the captives.

b. Rebuilding and restoring our broken city.

c. Being a righteous oak that reveals God's splendor.

d. Living shame-free.

e. Being in an everlasting covenant relationship with God himself.

PRAY

Pray for each other, for those still inside, and for those outside.

Final Thoughts and a Prayer

So here you are . . .

Listen to these powerful, stirring, and life-changing words, and think about the fact that St. Paul wrote these words while he was in prison, awaiting his execution at the hands of the state.

> What then are we to say about these things? If God is for us, who is against us? He who did not withhold his own Son, but gave him up for all of us, will he not with him also give us everything else? Who will bring any charge against God's chosen ones? It is God who justifies. Who is to condemn? It is Christ Jesus, who died, yes, who was raised, who is at the right hand of God, who indeed intercedes for us. Who will separate us from the love of Christ? Will hardship, or distress, or persecution, or famine, or nakedness, or peril, or sword? . . . No, in all these things we are more than conquerors through him who loved us.
>
> For I am convinced that neither death, nor life, nor angels, nor rulers, nor things present, nor things to come, nor powers, nor height, nor depth, nor anything else in all creation, will be able to separate us from the love of God in Christ Jesus our Lord. (Romans 8:31-39)

Make these words of St. Paul's your own, for the God he knew and served in his jail cell is exactly the same God who is in your cell with you now.

For I am certain that
neither prison wall,
nor segregation unit,
nor long-term sentence,
nor probation period,
nor family rejection,
nor bouts of depression,
nor crazy cellmate,
nor cruel officer,
nor gang, nor liquor store,
nor denied appeal,
nor lockdown,
nor lack of visits,
nor sleepless nights,
nor failed job interviews,
nor street corners,
nor anything else in all creation,
will be able to separate us
from the love of God
in Christ Jesus our Lord.

You are more than conquerors.
You are God's chosen, beloved ones.
Go and live like it!

You've heard from us. Now we'd love to hear from you!

The sole reason we wrote and produced this *Spiritual Survival Guide for Prison and Beyond* is that it might be helpful to you. And a big piece of this process has been collaboration—getting helpful input and feedback from current and former inmates. That means we want your feedback as well!

We'd love it if you let us know what parts you found inspiring, encouraging and instructive. We also want to know what sections you found confusing or boring. In addition, it would be helpful to hear how you've used this book for personal reading, as a conversation starter with your celly, or in a group setting. Let us know what difference it has made for you and others.

Feel free to share your comments, insights, personal experiences and wisdom with us. Because of our small size and limited budget, we at The Inside Out Network can't promise to respond directly to every letter we receive, or assist you legally or financially in any way. However, if you write to us, we promise to pray for you by name, carefully read everything you've written, and consider using your insights in a revised edition or second volume.

You can reach us at

The Inside Out Network
1006 Gillick St.
Park Ridge, IL 60068
ionillinois.net

God's amazing love,

Fred Nelson
and the people of The Inside Out Network